CLONFERT CATHEDRAL
Interior Elevation of East Windows

IRISH CHURCHES
AND
MONASTIC BUILDINGS

II
GOTHIC ARCHITECTURE
TO A.D. 1400

BY
HAROLD G. LEASK
M.Arch., Litt. D.; M.R.I.A., F.S.A.
F.R.S.A.I.; F.R.I.A.I.

Formerly Inspector of National Monuments
Office of Public Works
Dublin
(Author of " Irish Castles and Castellated Houses")

1990
DUNDALGAN PRESS (W. TEMPEST LTD.)
DUNDALK

PUBLISHED 1960 COPYRIGHT
SECOND IMPRESSION 1967
THIRD IMPRESSION 1990

PRINTED IN TWELVE POINT MONOTYPE OLD STYLE
BY
DUNDALGAN PRESS (W. TEMPEST) LIMITED, DUNDALK
REPUBLIC OF IRELAND

PREFACE

In the preface to the first volume of this work, a second was promised; its preparation had begun, indeed, before that preface was written. The second volume, it was intended, should deal with all Irish ecclesiastical architecture of the three hundred and fifty years or so from the first Irish appearance of the pointed arch to the Dissolution of the monasteries in the sixteenth century. As the work proceeded, however, it became clear that the original plan was somewhat too ambitious; it covered too long a period of time and too great a variety of buildings, all of interest. Of the two ways in which it could be accomplished—by the production of a very bulky and consequently expensive volume, or by very great compression of important sections together with a reduction in the number of illustrations—neither way seemed desirable.

These considerations led to a decision to produce a volume of moderate size but of lesser chronological scope than that originally planned. In such a work it would be possible to deal with the architecture of two centuries in a reasonably effective manner in both text and illustration. A.D. 1400 was selected as the limiting upper date. For several reasons this date is an obvious one. It marks the end of a half-century in which little building was done, a period of inactivity in strong contrast to the preceding two hundred years which were notable for remarkable activity in church and monastery construction. Moreover, towards the end of this pause the first signs of a new style were appearing. These very tentative signs belong properly to that style which, in turn, belongs to the succeeding century and merits, by reason of its very national character, a volume to itself. By such a volume the author hopes to complete—in due time and if his energies permit—his picture of Irish medieval architecture.

PREFACE

The first chapters deal with the coming of the Cistercian Order to Ireland and the fully-developed monastic plan which they brought with them. Those which follow treat of progressive stages in architectural development; of the Transition from round-arched Romanesque to full Gothic with its pointed arches; of the very individual Western school in which Transitional features lingered; of the Lancet style and the advent and development of window tracery.

The historical background is but lightly sketched. Where architecture is the primary concern there is little room for historical events unless these left their marks in stone. But some events did help or hinder architectural development and cannot be ignored. The happenings of the mid-fourteenth century, for instance, were of the latter kind and therefore receive more than passing mention.

Any presentation of architecture demands adequate illustration. This is specially true of Irish medieval building which has never, hitherto, been fully illustrated in any single book. But full illustration is not attainable within the small compass of a single volume of medium size; it is only possible in monographs on individual structures. (The number of such publications is regrettably small.) Therefore it has been necessary to select illustrations with care—to include only those absolutely essential to the purpose. Though many Irish buildings make attractive pictures, such views are too often of limited value as an aid to architectural analysis. The selection is mainly of the parts and details which best portray changes in style and fashion rather than one of pretty views. Much reliance is placed upon line drawings of the details—mouldings and the like—which no photograph can show but which, none the less, are necessary to supplement it. These details are bits and pieces—sometimes very small pieces—but all have significance in a proper understanding of the subject.

The author is conscious that in this book attainment falls short of intention. He hopes that, despite its defects, it may help to stimulate the reviving interest in the relics of Ireland's past.

ACKNOWLEDGMENTS

In the composition of this work I have drawn material from many sources, chief among them being the publications of the societies devoted to the study of Irish antiquities. To these, and especially the *Journal of the Royal Society of Antiquaries of Ireland* and the *Proceedings of the Royal Irish Academy*, I owe great debts here gratefully acknowledged. My obligation to the Commissioners of Public Works is even greater since it was in their service as Inspector of National Monuments that I had unique opportunities for the study of Irish medieval buildings. Moreover, they have generously given me permission to make full use of the archives of the National Monuments Branch of the Office of Public Works, an unrivalled collection of drawings, photographs and reports. For these privileges I am very grateful. To the officers of that branch, in particular to the Inspector, Mr. W. P. Le Clerc, and his colleague, Mr. L. de Paor, I also give thanks. Both have helped me greatly by the gift of notes and photographs as well as in the discussion of points of difficulty. I have also had the advantage of revisiting more than one ancient structure in the company of the Inspector.

Opportunities to visit buildings in Ulster were less numerous but the lack has been made up, in great measure, through the kindness of my friend, Mr. D. M. Waterman, of the Ancient Monuments Branch of the Ministry of Finance of Northern Ireland. He has been very helpful in supplying accurate details of medieval structures in that area and in the discussion of questions of detail and dating. I acknowledge this help with gratitude.

Of the books consulted few can be mentioned here—the titles of many of them will be found in the footnotes to the chapters—

but two, Champney's monumental *Ecclesiastical Architecture of Ireland* and Bond's *Gothic Architecture in England*, must be cited as chief among them. I owe more than I can express, however, to one work as yet unpublished: a thesis on Gothic Architecture in Ireland by my friend Dr. E. C. Rae, now of the University of Illinois. It was submitted in 1942 for the Degree of Doctor of Philosophy in the Graduate School of Harvard University. His thesis is the most definitive work on the subject yet to be done; more final than mine can be in the pages which follow. With extraordinary generosity Dr. Rae has allowed me to make use of his thesis. This I have done with much profit and for the privilege given I tender to him most sincere thanks.

I am indebted to the Rev. Professor Aubrey Gwynn, S.J. for several valuable and hitherto unnoticed historical references bearing upon the authorship and date of some structures (Tuam choir in particular), and to the Ven. Archdeacon J. L. Robinson for the loan of Butler's pre-restoration *Survey of Christ Church Cathedral, Dublin*—a rare work—and for his help in unravelling the building history of that edifice.

I am grateful for the considerable assistance given to me in the preparation of illustrations by my friends Mr. Brian Coghlan and Mr. Gearoid O hIceadha who were responsible, respectively, for Figures 4 and 63, and Figures 9, 10, 25, 26, 27, 35, 54 and 56.

Acknowledgment is also due to the late Mr. Thomas H. Mason who put his unique collection of photographs at my disposal thus making it possible to include some otherwise difficult to obtain. Plates: Frontispiece, IIIa, IV, VIb, XIb, XIV, XVIIa and XXI are from his collection. For the photograph from which Plate XXVIIIa was made I am indebted to Fräulein Waltraut Westen of Duisburg am Rhein. Those from which Plates VIa, VIIa, IX, XIIb, XIII, XVI, XXIIIb, XXVII and XXVIIIc were made are from the Office of Public Works collection and that for Plate XXVIa is the property of Bórd Fáilte Éireann. The Ministry of Finance of Northern Ireland has permitted me to use their print for Plate V. Mr. W. P.

A C K N O W L E D G M E N T S

Le Clerc kindly supplied the photographs for Plates XIX and XXIIIa. My thanks are also given to the following institutions for the permission to use blocks which are their property: The Royal Society of Antiquaries of Ireland: Figures 39, 40, 41, 48, 49, 50 and 58; The Royal Archæological Institute: Plates IIIb and c, XVa, XVIIIa and b, XXa and b, XXIIa and b, and Figures 21 and 24; The North Munster Archæological Society: my own blocks of Figures 1, 2, 3, 5, 6, 7, 8 and 15; The Louth Archæological Society: Plate XXVIb and Figure 3.

CONTENTS

I. THE CISTERCIANS IN IRELAND   1

    THE COMING OF THE CISTERCIANS   2

    THE ORGANIZATION OF THE ORDER   4

    MONKS AND LAY BRETHREN   5

    THE CISTERCIAN PLAN: GENERAL   5

II. THE AUGUSTINIAN AND OTHER ORDERS   19

III. TRANSITIONAL ARCHITECTURE, *circa* 1160-1200   25

IV. TRANSITIONAL ARCHITECTURE
    THE SCHOOL OF THE WEST   53

V. IRISH GOTHIC TO A.D. 1250   77

VI. IRISH GOTHIC IN THE LATER THIRTEENTH CENTURY   103

VII. IRISH GOTHIC IN THE FOURTEENTH CENTURY   123

VIII. SOME FEATURES OF CHURCHES AND MONASTERIES   137

    APPENDIX I. SHORT NOTICES OF BUILDINGS
    OMITTED FROM PRECEDING PAGES   145

    GLOSSARY   155

    INDEX   159

To
my friend
EDWIN CARTER RAE
I dedicate this volume
in grateful recognition
of the immense help his own work
in the same field
has been to me

LIST OF PLATES

St. Brendan's Cathedral, Clonfert, Galway:
Interior elevation of East wall - - *frontispiece*

I. Boyle Abbey Church, Roscommon: Interior
    Views: (*a*) Looking West from Nave;
    (*b*) North Transept from South-west *facing page* 32

II. do. (*a*) West elevation; (*b*) Capital in nave ,, 33

III. Mellifont Abbey, Louth: Lavabo
    (*a*) View from South, (*b*) Capitals - ,, 48

IV. Christ Church Cathedral, Dublin:
    Late Twelfth-century Capitals - - ,, 49

V. Grey Abbey Church, Down: West doorway - ,, 52

VI. Corcomroe Abbey Church, Clare:
    (*a*) Chancel, interior; (*b*) Archway to
    North chapel - - - - ,, 60

VIIa. do. View from South-west - - - ,, 61

VIIb. Cong Abbey Church, Galway: Capitals of
    East jamb of North doorway - - ,, 61

VIII. Cong Abbey, Galway: Capitals of North
    jamb of Slype doorway - - - ,, 64

IX. Drumacoo Church, Galway: South doorway - , 65

Xa & b. do. Capitals of East and West jambs - ,, 80

XIa. Christ Church Cathedral, Dublin: North
    arcade of Nave - - - - ,, 81

XIb. Dunbrody Abbey Church, Wexford: Interior
    looking East - - - - ,, 81

XII. St. Patrick's Cathedral, Dublin : Choir - - ,,
    looking East - - - - ,, 84

XIIIa. St. Mary's Church, New Ross, Wexford:
    East windows of Chancel - - - ,, 85

XIIIb. St. Patrick's Cathedral, Cashel, Tipperary:
Transept looking South   -   -   *facing page* 85

XIV. Graignamanagh Abbey Church, Kilkenny:
Processional doorway from South aisle
to Cloister   -   -   -   -   ,,   92

XVa. St. Brigid's Cathedral, Kildare: Exterior
of Nave   -   -   -   -   ,,   93

XVb. St. John's Priory Church, Kllkenny:
East windows   -   -   -   -   ,,   93

XVI. St. Patrick's Cathedral, Cashel, Tipperary:
North windows of choir   -   -   ,,   100

XVIIa.   do. Exterior view from South-west -   -   ,,   101

XVIIb.   do. Capitals in Transept   -   -   ,,   101

XVIIIa. St. Canice's Cathedral, Kilkenny: Exterior
view from South-west   -   -   -   ,,   108

XVIIIb.   do. Interior looking North-east and
South-east   -   -   -   -   ,,   108

XIX.   do. West doorway   -   -   -   ,,   109

XXa.   do. Tomb recess in North Transept -   -   ,,   112

XXb. Ardfert Cathedral, Kerry: Interior of Choir
looking South-east   -   -   -   ,,   112

XXIa. Ardfert Friary Church, Kerry: Interior of
Choir looking East   -   -   -   ,,   113

XXIb. Gowran Church, Kilkenny: Interior of Nave
looking West   -   -   -   -   ,,   113

XXIIa. Cloyne Cathedral, Cork: East side of South
Transept   -   -   -   -   ,,   128

XXIIb.   do. Gable of South Transept   -   -   ,,   128

XXIIIa. Gowran Church, Kilkenny: East window of
South aisle   -   -   -   -   ,,   129

XXIIIb. Castledermot Friary Church, Kildare:
Arcade of Transept chapels   -   -   ,,   129

XXIVa. Kilmallock Friary Church, Limerick:
East window   -   -   -   -   ,,   132

XXIVb. Adare Friary ("Black Abbey") Church,
Limerick: East window   -   -   ,,   132

XXVa. Kilkenny Friary (" Black Abbey ") Church:
South window of Transept - *facing page* 133

XXVb. Tuam Cathedral, Galway: East window - ,, 133

XXVIa. Drogheda, Louth, Dominican Friary: The
Magdalene Tower - - - ,, 140

XXVIb. Mellifont Abbey, Louth: Window in Chapter
House - - - - ,, 140

XXVII. do. Part of Cloister arcade, restored - ,, 141

XXVIIIa. Jerpoint Abbey Church: Credence niche and
Sedilia - - - - ,, 144

XXVIIIb. Ardmore Cathedral, Waterford:
Tomb recess - - - - , 144

XXVIIIc. Gowran Church, Kilkenny: Tomb recesses - ,, 144

LIST OF ILLUSTRATIONS

(Marginal drawings are indicated by *M*)

		page
1.	Jerpoint Abbey: Conjectural Restoration, Bird's-eye View	7
2.	Plan of a Cistercian Abbey in Ireland based on Jerpoint remains - - - -	9
3.	Mellifont Abbey: Plan - - - -	11
4.	Irish Cistercian Abbey Churches: Comparative Plans	13
5.	Baltinglass Abbey Church: Capitals - -	27
6.	Typical Windows: (*a* and *d*) Jerpoint Transept and Clearstorey; (*b* and *c*) Monasternenagh -	29
7.	Jerpoint Abbey Church: Capitals. The upper from Transept Chapels, the lower from east end of nave - - - - -	30
8.	Jerpoint Abbey Church: Nave Arcade and Clearstorey	31
9.	Boyle Abbey Church: East Window in chapel -	*M* 32
10.	do. Chapel Pier Bases - - -	*M* 33
11.	do. Bases and Spurs - - - -	*M* 33
12.	do. Mouldings of West window and door, etc. -	34
13.	do. Boyle Abbey: Capitals, early, in Nave -	*M* 34
14.	Capitals from Monasternenagh Abbey Church and O'Heyne's Church, Kilmacduagh - -	35
15.	Monasternenagh Abbey Church: West windows -	36
16.	Knockmoy Abbey Church: Presbytery details -	37
17.	Knockmoy Abbey Church: East window hoods -	*M* 38
18.	do. Nave Capitals - - - -	*M* 39
19.	Mellifont Abbey: Lavabo details - - -	40
20.	Christ Church Cathedral, Dublin: Triforium and Clearstorey of Transept - - -	44
21.	Limerick Cathedral: Plan - - -	46
22.	Inch Abbey Church: Transept Chapel piers -	48
23.	Cistercian Abbey Churches: East ends, comparative - (Grey and Corcomroe) - -	50

24. Killaloe Cathedral: Plan - - - - 55
25. do. Corbel capitals - - - - M 55
26. do. do. - - - - - M 56
27. do. Interior of East window - - - 57
28. Cong Abbey: Details - - - - 60
29. Ballintober Abbey Church: Interior looking east and Plan 62
30. do. an east window - - - - M 63
31. Killone Abbey Church: East windows - - 64
32. Banagher Church: Window in South wall - - 65
33. Inishmaine Abbey: Plan - - - - 66
34. do. East windows - - - - 68
35. do. Capitals to Chancel Arch piers - - 68
36. Kilmacduagh, O'Heyne's Church: East window - 69
37. do. Monastery: Plan - - - - 70
38. Clonfert Cathedral: East window - - - M 71
39. Inchcleraun, Temple More: East windows - - 72
40. Drumacoo Church: Plan - - - - 73
41. do. Inside Elevation of East wall - - 74
42. Christ Church Cathedral, Dublin: Nave Arcade Details 78
43. Christ Church and St. Patrick's Cathedrals, Dublin:
        Bays of arcades - - - - 80
44. Dunbrody Abbey Church: Corbels in Nave - - M 84
45. St. Mary's Church, New Ross: Window details - M 85
46. Graignamanagh Abbey Church: Processional
        Doorway details - - - - 88
47. Cashel Cathedral: Mouldings of grouped north
        windows of Choir - - - - M 90
48. Athassel Priory: Plan - - - - 96
49. do. West Doorway of Choir - - - 99
50. Kilkenny Cathedral : Plan - - - 104
51. do. Details of Crossing Piers and Nave arches - 107
52. do. do. of West doorway - - - M 108
53. Kilkenny, St. John's Priory Church: East window
        details - - - - - M 109
54. do. and Cashel Cathedral: Capitals with faces in foliage 109
55. Ardfert Cathedral: Elevation of East gable (After Hill) 112
56. East windows: Ennis and Kilkenny Friary Churches 119
57. Athenry Friary Church: Plan - - - 127
58. do. Windows in extended Chancel, etc. (a) in north
        aisle, (b and c) in north and south walls - 128

B

59. Kilkenny, " Black Abbey "; Tracery of South
    window - - - - - M 129
60. Fethard Abbey: Nave windows - - - M 129
61. Jerpoint Abbey Church: East window - - M 129
62. Mellifont Abbey Chapter House: Plan, etc. - 130
63. Claregalway Friary Church: Capital in nave aisle - M 130
64. Kilmallock Friary Church; Capital in Transept - M 130
65. Kilkenny, St. Francis' Friary: Tower - - 133
66. do. Capital in respond of Transept - - M 134
67. Tomhaggard Church: Window - - - M 136
68. Kilkenny Cathedral: Niche in Transept chapel - M 141
69. St. Mary's Church, New Ross: Piscina - - M 141
70. Corcomroe Abbey Church: Sedilia - - - 142
71. Kilkenny, St. Francis' Friary Church: Sedilia - 143
72. Fenagh " Abbey " Church: East window - - M 148
73. Rosconnell Church: East windows - - - 152
74. Arch Forms, Foliations, Roll sections, etc. - - 155
75. " Dog-tooth " and " Nail-head " ornaments - M 156
76. " Stiff-leaf " Capital, Ardfert Cathedral - - M 158
77. " Water-holding " Bases - - - - M 158

Chapter I

THE CISTERCIANS IN IRELAND

LONG before the Irish Romanesque had run its full course—even before it had reached its highest development at Clonfert—the brethren of the great monastic order of Citeaux, the Cistercians, had come to Ireland and were spreading through the country. Their earliest works have vanished save for some foundations at the mother house of Mellifont—remains of the church begun in the 1140's and consecrated in 1157. It was almost certainly on a French model and Romanesque in style.

The order was, however, to be the bearer of a new style, a phase in the developing architecture of Gothic Europe and the first to practise it in Ireland. Others of the great orders—to say nothing of the secular clergy—were to play their parts in architectural development later but the Cistercians take pride of place. It is true that the first great monastic rule, that of St. Benedict, was known and practised in Ireland as early as the seventh and eighth centuries, but it vanished in the Viking terror. In any case its buildings are not part of the Gothic story. Indeed, there survives in Ireland no Benedictine building of a date prior to *c.* 1200—with one possible (Romanesque) exception to be mentioned later—the first appearance of the Gothic pointed arch is in buildings raised by the Cistercian order.

The earliest monastic communities of Ireland, as in Gaul and Britain, housed themselves in groupings of the *laura* form. That is to say, of numerous separate dwellings—each the cell of an individual monk, living under self-imposed austerities—within an

I

enclosure and grouped around a church or churches and a few structures of common use. The idea of a common life under one roof, which had originated with St. Basil as early as the year 360, was crystallized by St. Benedict in the sixth century and, gradually, the Rule which he composed for his great monastery at Monte Cassino " became the law of monastic life of western Europe."[1] The Benedictine conception was of " a common life of uniform duty "; its aim " the growth in grace of a brotherhood, living under a common rule in obedience to an abbot."[2] Emulation in good works, rooted in humility and obedience, was its watchword.

It is obvious that a monastic life on these lines could not be lived in all completeness in a grouping of isolated cells; it called for a very different type of structure: church and cloister an integrated whole. This was the kind of establishment, an " abbey " in the European sense, that the Cistercians brought to Ireland.

THE COMING OF THE CISTERCIANS

It was sainted Malachy, bishop of Armagh from 1132 to 1136 and later bishop again of his original see of Connor, who first brought the Cistercians to Ireland. Long-sought reforms were in progress in the church in Ireland but Papal confirmation of the changes being made had not been obtained by 1139. The Irish bishops, therefore, dispatched Malachy to Rome " to secure for Armagh and Cashel the archbishop's pallium."[3] On his way to Rome about 1140 Malachy stayed for a time at Clairvaux where the great Bernard ruled the abbey, a daughter of that of Citeaux, head of the new order which was one of several offshoots from that of the Benedictines, and had come into being about thirty years earlier. At Citeaux and Clairvaux, under the abbots Stephen Harding and Bernard, there was practised a very literal and austere observance of the rule of St. Benedict. The Cistercian monk might eat no meat; the abbey buildings must be simple but soundly built and free from ornament; window glass was to be plain and paintings, except of wooden crucifixes, were forbidden; stone belfries were not to be built and those of timber were to be of moderate height; even vestments were to be as plain as might be compatible with dignity. Each Cistercian establishment was a self-contained unit having within the walls of its precinct not only church and cloister but workshops, barns, stables and the like. It was the ideal of the order, attained in most cases, that each abbey should be sited in a place remote from centres of population. Indeed, no village of lay folk was to be permitted to arise close to the abbey precinct.

It was this Cistercian life and just such an establishment that Malachy saw at Clairvaux. So much did this dedicated life attract him that he wished to join St. Bernard's monks and finish his days among them. But Pope Innocent II, to whom he preferred this request on his arrival in Rome, would not grant it. Considering the good bishop's services too valuable to the Irish church to be discontinued, the Pope denied Malachy his wish and sent him back home armed with legatine authority to convene a national synod which should regularize the request for the pallia. Malachy halted again at Clairvaux on his homeward journey and, this time, detached some members of his train and left them in St. Bernard's care to be trained and professed in the Rule of the Order. From Ireland he later sent others for the same purpose. About two years afterwards, c. 1142, these Irishmen with sufficient French monks to make up the customary conventual number, came to Ireland and were settled at Mellifont in the present county of Louth. Here, on the bank of the little river Mattock, Donagh O Carroll, prince of the locality of Uriel, gave a site and lands to the brethren. No abbey is built in a day or a year and it was not until 1157 that the church at Mellifont was consecrated. At least the eastern part must have been completed by that time. The gathering on that day of consecration was such as had not been seen in Ireland since the day at Cashel, twenty-three years before, when Teampull Chormaic was hallowed. Clerics and notables were present in great numbers. The primate of all Ireland officiated and with him were the archbishops of Dublin and Tuam, the Papal Legate from his see of Lismore and many other prelates. The High King, Murteach MacLochlain, was there, matching O Carroll's gift of three score ounces of gold and surpassing it with one of eight score cows. Dervorgilla, now penitent, was present and gave a gift of gold equal to that of the High King. Her husband, O Ruairc, was also there.

THE ORGANIZATION OF THE ORDER

This is not a history of monastic development but something must be said of the Cistercian system of colonization and affiliation and how the Order spread in Ireland, as elsewhere, with such astonishing rapidity. The monastic life provided centres of peace and order in a troubled world—not least so in its Irish corner—and this was, doubtless, a prime attraction to postulants. Hardly less attractive, in a country primarily agricultural, must have been the Cistercians' devotion to the cultivation of the soil. In the earlier generations the Order was immensely popular. As any abbey grew in size it could—with the permission of the General Chapter—send forth a band or bands of monks (each usually twelve in number with an abbot at its head) to colonize a house on some new site granted by a pious layman: prince, chief or king. Such a colony in turn, and within a very few years in some cases, could and often did send out its own colonies to other places. Each house of the Order was ruled by its own abbot and was subject, not to a bishop but to the abbot of the parent house and, ultimately, to the General Chapter of the Order. Thus all stemmed back to the parent of all, Citeaux, the head of the whole federation. Mellifont stood in this relation to most of the Irish houses but not to the nine which, through their Anglo-Norman founders, owed direct filial allegiance to some English parent abbey. Mellifont and its family; daughters, grand-daughters and so on, totalled twenty-five by *c.* 1200 and there were five of Anglo-Norman foundation by the same date. The grand total, including minor houses—perhaps short-lived—

and some which may have been no more than cells was forty by 1272, the year in which Hore, the last of the Cistercian abbeys, was founded.

MONKS AND LAY BRETHREN

In each Cistercian abbey, as in the houses of some of the other orders, the brethren were divided into two classes: monks (*monachi*) and lay brothers (*conversi*). The duties of the former, who was literate but not necessarily always a priest, lay mainly in the church and cloister. The *conversus*, on the other hand, was a lay-man, a novice duly professed in the Order but not necessarily nor usually lettered, whose main business was manual labour in work-shop or field. While the monk spent the greater part of his time in the church in prayer and the recital of the offices, and in cloister upon clerical work, the lay brother's day was given up to hard bodily labour. Certain of the monks held official positions connected with the business of the house. Of such were the cellarer, the kitchener, the novice master and so forth. Fuller consideration of the inhabitants of an abbey and their activities would be irrelevant to the theme of monastic architecture and planning.

THE CISTERCIAN PLAN; GENERAL

In all essentials the lay-out of a Cistercian abbey is a standard one modified only by circumstances of size and site. It is the model upon which the establishments of the other orders of monks and friars came to be based, with minor variations of one sort or another which will engage attention later in these pages.

It is convenient to make use of the plan of Jerpoint Abbey, Co. Kilkenny (which is more complete than others of the early period) as a basis for the study of the Cistercian plan in detail. Though by no means the largest Irish abbey of the Order, nor the earliest in date—Jerpoint is a grand-daughter of Mellifont—it embodies in fair completeness the essential features of the Cistercian plan as found in Ireland. The bird's-eye view of a conjectural restoration of Jerpoint (1) and the plan based upon it (2) showing the buildings as at *c.* 1200 will serve as illustration.

At Jerpoint there remain to-day the whole of the church (minus the south arcade and aisle of the nave), the lower storey of the eastern range as well as parts of the south buildings; the western range, however—as in almost all of the Irish houses—has disappeared. There is some reason to believe that it may have been the first building to be erected, in some cases, to house the *conversi* engaged upon the construction of the abbey. It is possible, therefore, that this section may have been rapidly and perhaps rather impermanently built, a circumstance which could account for its frequent disappearance. There are some abbeys, however (Dunbrody and Inch, for instance) where it seems never to have been built. In all abbey establishments there were other buildings of mundane use: guest-house, school, granary, barns and byres, brew-house and bake-house, the almonry, etc. These were usually in the outer court or *curia*. Unfortunately, at no Irish Cistercian abbey site can there now be found any remains of these essentials excepting gate-houses at Mellifont and Dunbrody, and a bake-house at Inch. Of a building more closely associated with the cloister—the infirmary—there are more fragments or indications. The south-east wing at Mellifont seems to have been a hall with aisles, probably the infirmary; the buildings at Inch, Graigna-managh, Kilcooly and Holy Cross lying to the south-east of the cloister, are almost certainly infirmaries. At Holy Cross a small building with three apartments on each floor between the infirmary and the cloister proper was probably separate quarters for the abbot: his lodging. Most of these remnants, however, belong to later centuries than do the church and claustral buildings.

The Church

The church is, of course, the most important and considerable building of the group. It is cruciform in plan with a short, unaisled presbytery, a transept with chapels—usually two or three in

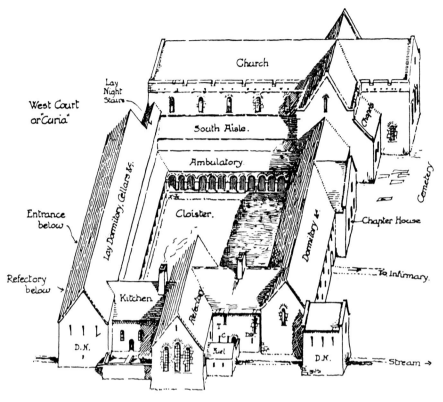

Church

Lay
Night
Stairs

West Court
or "Curia"

South Aisle.

Ambulatory.

Chapel

Cemetery

Entrance
below

Cloister.

Dormitory

Chapter House

Refectory
below

Kitchen

Refectory

To Infirmary.

D.N.

Fuel

D.N.

Stream →

Lay Dormitory. Cellars &c.

T. Treasury   C. Calefactory   D.S.: Day Stairs.

1. BIRD'S-EYE VIEW OF JERPOINT ABBEY CHURCH
CONJECTURAL RESTORATION

NOTE—This partly conjectural picture was made in 1939; later study and recent excavations show that it should be amended in some particulars. The original church, for instance, is unlikely to have had wall-walks and parapets; plain over-sailing eaves are more probable in an Irish church of *c.* 1200. It is possible, also, that the eastern limb was lower than is shown. In the east wall of the south end of the dorter range three small pointed windows survive, together with a doorway below them. This has a segmental-pointed backarch. These features are of the thirteenth century and, therefore, this part of the range—and perhaps the whole of it—is of that period as is the refectory which has a single pointed light in the east wall.

Excavations have defined, more clearly, the drain or sewer in the position shown and have, in addition, revealed the foundations of a small structure projecting into the garth from the centre of the north arcade of the ambulatory. The purpose of this building is obscure but was certainly of sufficient importance to require that it should be rebuilt when, in the fifteenth century, the south aisle of the church was demolished and the ambulatory moved northwards.

number—to the east of each arm, and a nave with north and south aisles. The first church of the Order in Ireland—at the mother-house of Mellifont, consecrated in 1157—was doubtless of this plan.   It was displaced, however, by another built *c.* 1200 and the only vestiges of the original edifice remaining are the foundations of the side and end-walls of a short, square-ended presbytery, together with those of the transeptal chapels (3).   These were very small and numbered three in each arm of the transept.   The central chapel in each group was square-ended but its neighbours were apsidal: the only appearance in Ireland of this very continental feature.   Perhaps it was Robert, the French monk-architect sent by Bernard from Clairvaux, who introduced it at Mellifont. Though it is not certain that Bernard's abbey church had apses at this time the feature was known and used in France in the previous century[4] and Robert could have seen it.   The apse was too foreign for acceptance by Irish church builders who—like most of the British also—preferred and adhered to the square finish.   After the departure of Robert from Mellifont (the French brethren had left there before his arrival) the apse appears no more in Ireland. Even the examples of it at Mellifont disappeared beneath the second church built there about half a century later.   The first had no central belfry (Boyle and Grey abbeys are exceptions, and a tower may have been intended over the crossing at Monasternenagh); the Cistercians normally eschewed such vanities in the early years at least.   The roof of the nave ran level and unbroken from west to east as far as the arch of the presbytery.   The transept roofs, generally of a height equal with that of the nave, intersected it, and the roof of the presbytery was usually of lower elevation. Wide arches spanned the transept openings.   Westwards from the crossing (the space corresponding to the transept) lay the arcades between the nave and aisles with a variable number of arches: six at Jerpoint, eight at its parent, Baltinglass, and at Boyle, seven at Graignamanagh and as few as four in some other churches. An exception, Grey Abbey (Down) had no aisles.   The principal

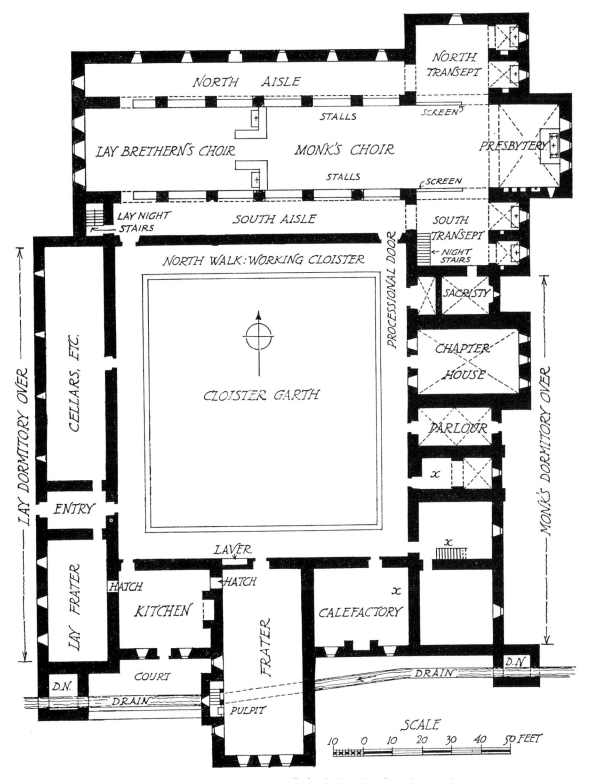

2. Plan of a Cistercian abbey in Ireland; based on Jerpoint remains

windows were in the east and west gables and that of the north transept and in the clearstorey over the nave arcades. It is a peculiarity of several Irish Cistercian churches, and of other (parish) churches built under the influence of the Order, that the clearstorey windows were over the pillars of the arcade and not, as is more usual, over the arch centres (8). This placing secured a small reduction in the wall height and is to be found in some west of England churches where, apparently, this was the object aimed at. These windows, at Jerpoint and Boyle, are round-headed and widely splayed inwards.

At most of the Irish abbey churches, as at Jerpoint, the presbytery is very short. It is there barrel-vaulted and originally had three small, round-headed windows behind the high altar. Also vaulted are the transept chapels but over the remainder of the church there were roofs of timber. In the south-west angle of the transept was a flight of steps rising to the still existing doorway of the dorter or dormitory. This was the night-stairs by which the monks came and went to and from the recital of the night offices in choir. A similar stairs at the west end of the south aisle served the lay brothers for a similar, less frequently demanded duty.

About midway in its length the nave was divided into two parts by a screen wall or walls. In the Irish cases (Monasternenagh, Holy Cross and Corcomroe) where this is a single wall carried to the whole height of the church, it is usually of later date than the rest of the building. At Jerpoint, however, the arrangement is less simple and more, though not completely, in accordance with the usual practices in the churches of the Order. This was to cut off a bay, or even two bays of the nave forming a retro-choir for aged and infirm monks, beneath a rood-loft. The eastern wall was the pulpitum, for on it stood two lecterns for the reading of the Gospel and the Epistle. The western wall supported the Rood, the great crucifix. This construction divided the choir of the monks, on the east—extending to the presbytery—from that of the lay brothers on the west. The wooden stalls of the monks, in several ranks, faced each other across the choir with their backs to the aisles and transepts. At Jerpoint and its parent, Baltinglass, low stone walls

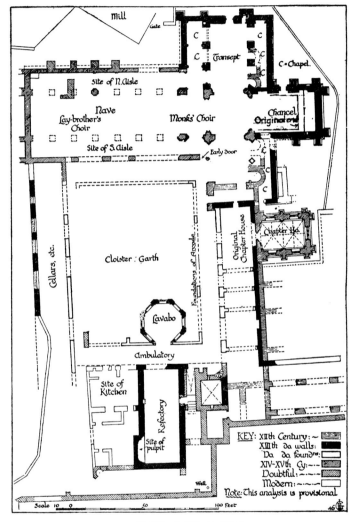

3. Mellifont Abbey: Plan

Since this plan was made there have been further discoveries not shown upon it: (*a*) of pseudo crypts under and outside the west end of the church, and (*b*) of the existence of an open passage from south to north and *east* of the west range ("Cellars, etc."), marked at the south end by the short wall shown hatched. The west ambulatory lay, therefore, east of this passage and the garth was narrower from east to west than is shown (see pp. 17 and 43).

between the pillars of the arcade—perpyn walls (8)—enclosed the choirs on each side at the backs of the stalls and timber screens served the same purpose across about two-thirds of the width of the transept openings. Timber screens, it is believed, crossed the aisles about half-way in their length. The stallwork returned at right angles at the pulpitum wall and here, to the right and left, respectively, of the choir entry, sat the abbot and prior facing the high altar.

The western part of the nave was the choir of the lay brothers, with similar stallwork and backing against the perpyn walls. It seems probable that, in accordance with Cistercian practice, at Jerpoint the western screen of the retrochoir (used by the infirm monks) lay between the two pillars west of the L-shaped walls shown on the plan. Against it would have stood the nave altar flanked by two doors. This arrangement—especially in view of the fact that the perpyn walls stop short of the western responds of the south arcade to allow access to the aisles—seems to leave little room for the lay brethren, but about sixty could have been accommodated in double-ranked stalls. It is not known to what use the north aisle was put but the presence of a doorway central in the wall, an original feature at Baltinglass and perhaps taking the place of an original opening at Jerpoint, suggests that the laity may have been admitted to this aisle.

The south aisle served at least as an internal passage. At its east end, in most Cistercian churches, a wide and important doorway opened southwards into the cloister ambulatory. Through this, the main connection between church and cloister, passed the Sunday procession after visiting all the altars in the church, to visit in turn all parts of the claustral buildings. The procession reentered the church near the west end of the south aisle to form up in two ranks in the lay choir before passing into choir again through the screen doors and the choir entry in the pulpitum. Over the nave screen stood the great crucifix—the Rood—and over the

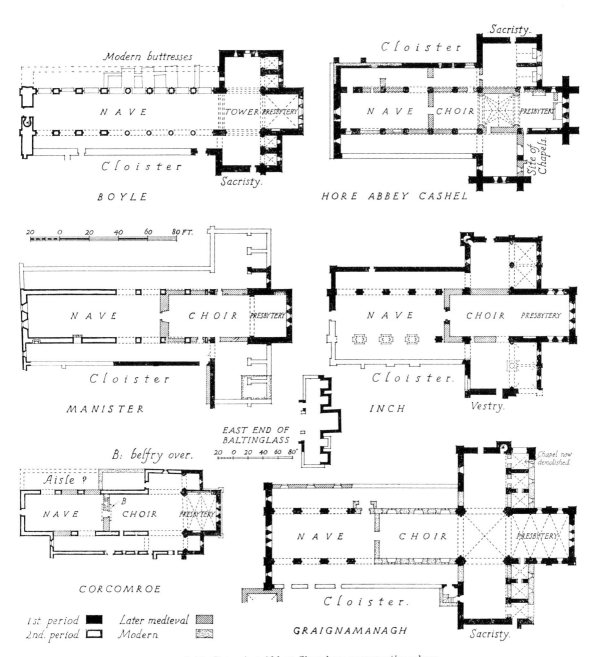

Modern buttresses

NAVE   TOWER   PRESBYTERY

Cloister

Sacristy.

BOYLE

Sacristy.

Cloister

NAVE   CHOIR   PRESBYTERY

Site of Chapels.

HORE ABBEY CASHEL

20   0   20   40   60   80 FT.

NAVE   CHOIR   PRESBYTERY

Cloister

MANISTER

NAVE   CHOIR   PRESBYTERY

Cloister.

INCH   Vestry.

EAST END OF BALTINGLASS

20   0   20   40   60   80'

B: belfry over.

Aisle ?

B

NAVE   CHOIR   PRESBYTERY

CORCOMROE

Chapel now demolished.

NAVE   CHOIR   PRESBYTERY

Cloister.

GRAIGNAMANAGH   Sacristy.

1st period ■   Later medieval ▨
2nd period □   Modern ▦

4.   Irish Cistercian Abbey Churches: comparative plans

pulpitum the Gospel and Epistle lecterns on the level of the loft
over the retrochoir and chapels.

Comparative plans of some Irish Cistercian abbey churches,
together with the eastern part of that at Baltinglass, are grouped
in (4).

The Claustral Buildings

In Ireland, as elsewhere, the Cistercian cloister normally lay to
the south of the church.   The only known Irish exception is at
Hore, Cashel (Tipperary), the last abbey built (1272), where
questions of water supply and drainage may have operated to
cause the change from the normal practice.   In northern latitudes
there is a distinct practical advantage in the southward position,
in that it would provide a sun-warmed centre for the life of the
brethren.   Backing to the church—which would overshadow and
chill a northern cloister—it would be sheltered also from the east
and west by the other buildings.   As there were few fireplaces in
any abbey structure of the Order it must have been a matter of
importance to make full use of the sun's warmth.

The Cloister

Round about the cloister court or garth ran the monastery's
main artery of communication: the ambulatory or cloister walk.
It was open towards the garth, with an arcade or maybe no more
than a wooden structure between.   Its roof was a " lean-to "
against the surrounding buildings.   At its north-east corner was the
processional doorway already mentioned.

The East Range

Abutting on the gable of the south transept and extending
southwards is the east or Dorter range.   On the ground floor is a
sacristy, entered from the transept, and a store—probably for the
books used in the cloister—with a door to the east walk.   At Jerpoint
both these apartments were vaulted.   Next in order is the Chapter

House or Room, also vaulted and projecting eastwards from the range. Here, as the name indicates, there was read every day a chapter of the Rule of the Order. It was the venue of many other gatherings of the brethren. Two windows flanked a doorway to the ambulatory and three windows in the east gable provided the only light. Further south is a vaulted passage which, at Jerpoint, appears to have served as the way from the cloister to the monks' cemetery which usually lay to the east of the church and the Dorter range. The use of the succeeding apartments to the south is not certain. They may have served as the Novice House, but at either of the two points marked " X " on the plan (or alternatively at the third " X " in the south range) was the Day Stairs leading up to the Dorter. This very important apartment, at Jerpoint nearly 120 feet in length, extended over the whole length of the range. Here slept the monks and—in the earliest practice of the Rule—the abbot amongst them, in an open, undivided room. In later times cubicles were provided and the abbot had his own separate and distinct quarters.

The South Range

Parallel with the church, across the cloister from it and closing the rectangle were placed the buildings of most mundane use. Adjoining the Dorter range was the Warming House or Calefactory, the one apartment, excepting the Kitchen, in which a fireplace was provided. Here, at certain appointed hours, the monks might meet by a fire and engage in conversation. It was entered from the ambulatory and had a small external courtyard in which was a fuel shed or store. The central room was the monks' dining hall, the Refectory or Frater. That at Jerpoint was over 60 feet in length and 27 feet wide. The Jerpoint example, and those extant in whole or part at Grey, Inch, Mellifont and Graignamanagh abbeys, stand at right angles to the range but in other houses the frater lay parallel to the church. This was the case at six of them: Boyle, Dunbrody, Knockmoy, Monasternenagh, Hore and Holy Cross.

A thickening of the west walls of the fraters of the first-named four and of the south walls at Dunbrody and Knockmoy accommodated the raised pulpit for the Reader: the brother who, at each meal, read homilies and the like to the silent monks at the tables. In a niche beside the Frater doorway in the south walk would be the Laver, the basin for washing hands before and after meals. This was the case in many abbeys but in some a separate building was provided—in the garth before the Frater door—as at Mellifont and Dunbrody. (Only foundations remain in the latter place.) A hatchway or " turn "—through which food was served—in the west wall communicated directly with the Kitchen, which did double duty in serving, through another " turn," the Frater of the Lay brethren in the end of the west range adjoining.

The West Range

In this wing, north from the lay frater which filled its southern end, were the cellars of the house, the main entry to the buildings and the cellarer's parlour or business room. All these were on the ground floor; on the upper floor and running the whole length of the range was the dorter of the lay brethren. At the southern extremities of both dorters were the necessaria: the sanitary accommodations. A stream of water was directed through both, passing by the Frater (under it at Jerpoint) and the Kitchen: a sewer or drain.

The Ambulatories

The primary purpose of these four covered walks was to give sheltered communication between all parts of the monastery but the north walk, next to the church, was less essential for this purpose. It could be, and in some houses, certainly was used as a working space: as an open-air scriptorium for instance. The lean-to roofs of all these walks were supported by arcades, walls with windows or maybe timber posts only. The remains extant at Jerpoint, though all round-arched, are of fifteenth century date but perhaps a copy of older work. The arcades at Bective and Holy Cross are also late but Mellifont had a stone-pillared arcade from an early date and at Baltinglass some stone fragments of thirteenth century design have been found. At no other Irish Cistercian abbeys does there now remain clear evidence of the existence of arcades of stone in the thirteenth century or earlier, though foundations of the low walls on which such arcades might have stood have been traced at a number of Irish cloisters. (A curious additional western walk, not roofed in, was revealed in recent excavations at Mellifont and will be dealt with in the description of the plan of that house at p. 43.)

1. Thompson: *English Monasteries*, Camb. (1913), p. 3.
2. *ibid.*, p. 4.
3. Curtis: *A History of Ireland*, Dublin (1936), p. 43.
4. Clapham: *Romanesque Architecture in Western Europe*, Oxford (1936), p. 82, cites N-D du Port, Clermont, as having rounded chapels substituted for square in the eleventh century.

Chapter II

THE AUGUSTINIAN AND OTHER ORDERS IN IRELAND

A Brief Account

PRIDE of place was given in the first chapter to the Cistercians and to the monastic plan which they were the first to introduce into Ireland. On the first page brief allusion was made to the other orders and the parts they were to play in the development of Irish ecclesiastical architecture. That architecture is the primary topic of the pages which follow; ecclesiastical history, important though it be in itself or in another context, is of secondary importance in this one. Nevertheless it cannot be ignored; something, however brief and general, must be said regarding the advent, the roles and structures of the other orders of monks and friars which took root in and flourished throughout Ireland in the thirteenth century.

The Irish activities of one, indeed, began much earlier; the monks following the Rule of St. Benedict appeared here perhaps as early as the seventh century. But their establishments were apparently destroyed during the ferocious raids of the Norse Vikings some two hundred years later. Before these catastrophies, and when the Benedictines came to Ireland again later, they had much influence upon the Irish Church and supplied bishops to more than one diocese, including the see of Dublin.[1] But we know nothing of the architectural form of the monasteries which they founded or re-founded, though there were certainly some of the latter. One was the abbey of Erinagh, *alias* Carrig, in Lecale, part of the present county of Down; an abbey there was destroyed by John de Courcy when he invaded Ulster in 1177. Even of the foundations made for Benedictines by the conquerors at various places there remain no traces with but one certain and one possible exception. The first is the abbey of Fore, in Westmeath (p. 47) and the second the eastern part of Jerpoint abbey church (p. 28).

Very important from the architectural viewpoint are the Canons Regular of St. Augustine. Like the Cistercians, they appear in Ireland in the twelfth century. It seems to be very probable that it was Malachy who first introduced the *Regula Augustini* into the fabric of the church he was helping to reform.[2] However this may be, the earlier Irish monasteries undoubtedly submitted, eventually, to the new rule. These submissions may account for the very large number—over two hundred—listed by the antiquaries Ware and Archdall, as Augustinian. These writers allocated to the Order almost all of the early Irish foundations. Many of them were small and some, indeed, may have vanished long before the acceptance of a new rule became obligatory. Some, like Glendalough or Kilmacduagh, were large and sprawling in lay-out, but even of the thirty or so of the Augustinian houses surviving, in whole or part, only eight are of really large size.

The Rule had considerable popular appeal. Though the Canons dwelt together in cloisters they came into closer contact with the people than did the Cistercian brethren. Their service of the parish churches round about their houses kept them in close touch with ordinary life. These houses were often educational centres and supported hospitals for the sick. Many were notable as houses of hospitality for travellers.

The church plan of an Augustinian monastery was not invariable. At Christ Church, Dublin, the choir was aisled and there were transeptal chapels; at Athassel, on the other hand, the eastern limb was long and unaisled, the typical form of choir in Canons' churches in Ireland.

Few of the Canons' houses retain claustral buildings. Where these survive—as at Athassel (Tipperary) and Kells (Kilkenny) for instance, they are to the south of the church and follow the Cistercian plan except in details to be dealt with later (p. 97). With the exception of Cong (Galway) the western houses of the Order are on a smaller scale than the great Anglo-Norman foundations in Kilkenny, Tipperary and Meath. At some of them there do not appear to have been complete, enclosed cloisters—an eastern wing only survives. Other churches had but transept-like wings.

The mendicant orders—the Friars Minor and Friars Preachers, Franciscan and Dominican—played a very considerable role in the Irish architectural scene. Both arrived in Ireland quite early in the thirteenth century, indeed, within a very few years of the deaths and canonizations of their founders. The Franciscans came in 1232; the Dominicans perhaps six years earlier. Both took root in or close to the towns which were developing under the Anglo-Normans. By the year 1260 the number of the houses of the Friars Minor was thirty and of the Dominicans sixteen; ultimately there were seventy-seven of the former and forty-seven of the latter. The Franciscan rule of poverty need not be stressed; nor need the close contact of the brethren with the people. Necessarily, lack of means had its effect upon the architecture of the Order; it was as simple as would be compatible with dignity. The churches were at first plain rectangles divided almost equally into a choir for the brethren and a nave for the laity. Later, as more space was required to accommodate the latter, an aisle was added to the nave and often a wing (loosely called a transept) in addition. It usually had sub-altars also. Both aisle and " transept " were on the opposite side of the church to the domestic buildings which, in Cistercian fashion, lay south of the church. Of these domestic buildings none datable to the thirteenth century remain. Indeed, it is doubtful if there were complete cloisters attached to the earlier churches; plain buildings on no regular plan possibly sufficed. Many of the earliest foundations have vanished beneath the buildings of the cities and towns in or near which they were erected. Where there are any remains datable to before *c.* 1260 they consist of the church fabric only. Of these survivals there will be much to say in later chapters. The same observations also apply to the Dominican remains.

Next in importance to the Franciscans and Dominicans, but later in appearance, were the Black Friars—Eremites or Hermits of St. Augustine, or Austin Friars—also a mendicant order. Antiquaries have sometimes confused them with the Dominicans for the reason that the latter at one time also wore a black habit. A case in point is Clonmines (Wexford) which has been credited to the Friars Preachers instead of to the Hermits, who were the actual occupiers. The Order was founded under papal authority and was devoted to the papal interest. It had its origin in a bull dated 1243 issued by Innocent IV and was furthered by his successor, Alexander IV. There were over a score of its establishments in Ireland, the earliest (Dublin) was founded in 1259 but few of the others belong to the thirteenth century. Half a dozen are datable in the 1300's; the remainder are fifteenth-century foundations. Some survivors of the earlier periods will be described in later pages.

Less important, architecturally speaking, are the Carmelites. They are said to have appeared in Ireland *c.* 1260 and had at one time twenty-four houses in the country. Almost all of them have disappeared.

Even less numerous were the houses of the Cross-Bearers or Crutched Friars. Only one of the twelve establishments with which the Irish branch of the Order is credited remains; that at Newtown-Trim (Meath) its buildings broken and much altered in post-Dissolution times.

At the three dozen places where there were houses of the Tertiaries—the Third Order of St. Francis—there are few traces of any structures. Such buildings as exist all belong to the fifteenth century and are therefore not within the scope of this volume.

There were seven Irish monasteries of the Order of Prémontré—
the Premonstratensians—but only one (Trinity Island, Loch Cé,
Roscommon) still stands, ivy-enshrouded, on its lake islet. Though
following the Augustinian Rule in most things the Premonstratensian Canons had an organization of affiliated houses on the
Cistercian model and, like the latter order, set up their establishments generally in remote places. Architecturally they seem to
have exerted little influence.

The remains of the Irish establishments of the once mighty
Knights Templars, or those of their successors, the Hospitallers,
have vanished, or are hardly recognizable now. The Trinitarian
Order had but one Irish house. Its church still survives at Adare
(Limerick) restored and in use as a parish church. Foundations for
female religious are rare in the period. About a score are credited
to Canonesses of St. Augustine and one to Cistercian nuns. Of the
buildings of the former only one remains in a fairly complete state
(Killone, Clare, p. 63) and at the site of another, the once famous
educational house of Gracedieu (Dublin), some small fragments of
walling lie to the north of what was obviously a cloister court. The
Cistercian nunnery of Down has quite disappeared.

It would, of course, be easy to expand this short and generalized chapter very greatly in a number of ways: by accounts of
the special aims, objects and history—in Ireland—of the various
orders, for instance. But, as has been said already, this volume is
primarily devoted to the study of architecture upon which the
minutiæ of monastic history have had little discernible influence.
Yet history, ecclesiastical or political, is not excluded from the
chapters following; it makes its appearance wherever it has—or
seems to have had—a bearing on the development of Irish architecture in general, on a local style or on particular structures.

1. de Varebeke: *J.R.S.A.I.*, vol. lxxx (1950), pp. 92-98.
2. Dunning: " The Arroasian Order in Medieval Ireland," *Ir. Hist. Studies*, Vol. IV,
No. 16.

Chapter III

TRANSITIONAL ARCHITECTURE

Circa 1160 to 1200

IN the living medieval architecture of western Europe development was continuous. In one sense, therefore, any phase of it may be called transitional. Writers on English architecture, however, have applied the term specifically to the stage in architectural development in which round-arched Romanesque and its motives gave place, gradually, to the full Gothic style with its pointed arches, distinctive mouldings and sculpture. The term is equally aplicable in Ireland where western English architectural influences were strong at the time. Moreover, its use is justified by the vigorous and rapid growth and change in Irish building during the period.

In Britain the pointed arch made its first appearance about the middle of the twelfth century and the new form had virtually displaced the older one by *c.* 1200. The Cistercians introduced the new fashion into Ireland and in this introduction no lengthy time-lag between the English and Irish appearances need be assumed since the Order in Ireland was at that time in close and sympathetic contact with others of its members in Britain and beyond. There-fore the first steps in the Transition in Ireland may be dated to before *c.* 1170. On the other hand the Irish development was slower and it was not until *c.* 1230 (or later in the west where the chevron motive persisted, cf. Drumacoo church) that the earlier style entirely ceased to influence ecclesiastical building. Moreover, the native Romanesque died hard; it was still a living style in

25

regions remote from Cistercian and Anglo-Norman influence in the last decades of the twelfth century (cf. Annaghdown, vol. I, p. 157).

The most characteristic examples in the earliest stage of the Transition are the Cistercian abbey churches of Baltinglass (Wicklow), Jerpoint (Kilkenny) and Boyle (Roscommon). Baltinglass belongs to the first generation of Mellifont's daughters and was colonized from the mother house in 1148 or soon thereafter. Its royal founder was Dermott MacMurrough, the king of Leinster, he who invited the assistance of the Anglo-Normans to recover his kingdom: " Dermott of the Foreigners," the " Diarmaid na nGall " of the annalists. He was apparently sufficiently wealthy to found and erect (about 1154) a small Augustinian monastery at Ferns (Wexford), his royal seat. This was before his expulsion from the country (1167) and it is difficult to believe that work at his larger foundation of BALTINGLASS had not been at least begun before the latter date. The eastern part of the abbey church there, altered as it is, still retains both the broad, round arches of the openings to the vanished transept. To each arm of this, as recent excavations (1955) have shown, there were two chapels not merely divided from one another by single walls, in the usual fashion, but each in a separate projection: a unique arrangement (4). The bases of the transept archways are distinctively Irish (Vol. I, 49g) bulbous in form in two cases. In these, perhaps, an Irish mason—a *conversus ?*—made his humble protest against Cistercian austerity. The certainly later S. arcade of choir and nave, eight bays in length, remains. Its piers are alternately of square and circular plan and all but one rise from perpyn walls now broken away in the openings. Crowning the piers are capitals, also square, boldly scalloped over the cylindrical pillars and more shallowly over those that are square. Much simplified Irish motives decorate them all (5). The abaci are square-edged and chamfered below a bevelled groove and the bluntly-pointed arches—typical of the early Transition— slightly chamfered at the edges, have plain chamfered hood-mouldings on the inner face only. Sited over the pillars are the clearstorey windows represented now only by the lower parts of the inside splays. Central in the N. aisle are the lower jambs of a

5. Baltinglass Abbey Church: capitals

doorway in three orders. Of these the inner and outer have angle
rolls bounded by two angular fillets and that in the middle has bold
chevrons overriding a small angle roll. There are also the remains
of the jambs of the processional doorway from the S. aisle to the
cloister, shallowly moulded and decorated in the native fashion.
This doorway and the transept and presbytery (on an axis oblique
to that of the nave) are the earliest parts of the church. The nave
is probably of *c.* 1165. Its features bear a remarkable resemblance
to those of Buildwas abbey church (Salop), begun *c.* 1155-60.[1]
and doubtless complete by 1170, a house which had many later
(and possibly earlier) connexions with Irish Cistercian history.

JERPOINT, the second example, is itself a daughter of
Baltinglass from which it received a colony in 1180.[2] A conjectural
plan of this abbey, based upon its remains, has been used in the
preceding chapter to typify the Cistercian lay-out; its architecture
is now to be described. A rough barrel-vault covers the very short
presbytery and above it there appears to have been a chamber
beneath a high-pitched stone roof of the Irish type. Still visible in
the E. wall are two jambs of the three original windows, round-
headed lights, externally about two feet wide and four high, with a
border decoration of chevrons. It is possible that the central
light—displaced by the fourteenth-century three-light window
(61)—was higher and wider than its companions.

A chamfered string-course with decorations of pointed bosses
forms a sill and another, at a higher level, simply moulded, rises
over the arches as a hood. All this work is Romanesque rather than
of the Transition; a remark also applicable to the transept windows (6a) which, though of unusually wide proportion, have
inclining jambs in the Irish fashion. These circumstances suggest
strongly that the presbytery and transept, in their original form,
are of an earlier date than the W. limb of the church which is
Transitional and of *c.* 1170-80. It is not impossible that the eastern
section of the church may have been begun by another Order (not
named but probably Benedictine); may be, indeed, the not specifi-

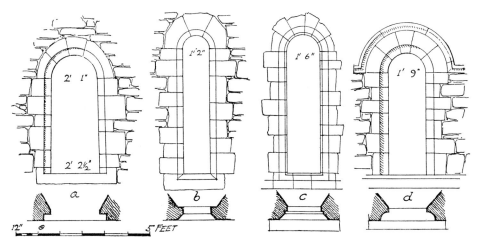

6. Typical windows: (*a* and *d*) Jerpoint transept and clearstorey; (*b* and *c*) Monasternenagh

cally identified " Convent of Ossory " founded and endowed in 1158 by King MacGillapatrick of Ossory. The conflict in the recorded foundation and colonization dates could be resolved by the acceptance of the architectural evidence. It seems certain that the first-projected church was to be of cruciform, aisleless plan. Whether it had chapels is uncertain—their arches, at least, agree in style with the nave work and the chapels, which are barrel-vaulted, may be Cistercian additions. These arches are chamfered and rise from capitals (7) reminiscent of Baltinglass nave but somewhat more boldly carved with motives still Irish in type. The jambs have angle rolls, each with several broad yet shallow fillets which give a fluted effect.

The arches to the transept were removed to make way for the tower inserted in the fifteenth century but their springing points are visible. The archways to the aisles are contemporary with the nave arcades. Only the N. arcade remains complete, but its companion was doubtless of the same design as its eastern, surviving, bay indicates. The pillars are short and, as at Baltinglass, rise from the remnants of the perpyn walls (8). In the four eastern bays cylindrical and square-planned pillars alternate; the western pillars

7. Jerpoint Abbey Church: capitals. The upper three from transept chapels; the lower from east end of nave

are square in plan with engaged angle shafts. The capitals vary in design: of block form to the square pillars (decorated and V-notched to the E. respond and scalloped to the others) and a plain square block, above scalloped flutings, crowns the round pillars. All the abaci, excepting that to the eastern respond, are hollow-chamfered. The arches are blunt-pointed and have hood-mouldings on both faces, chamfered, and the round-headed windows of the clear-storey are sited over the pillars. So strong is the likeness to the Baltinglass arcade that the presence of the same workmen at each abbey in succession may be inferred. Three large, round-headed windows fill the west gable. In addition to partial destruction in relatively modern times the Jerpoint church has suffered changes: the insertion of the E. window and of others in the chapels; the erection of the tower (to be dealt with in its place later); the

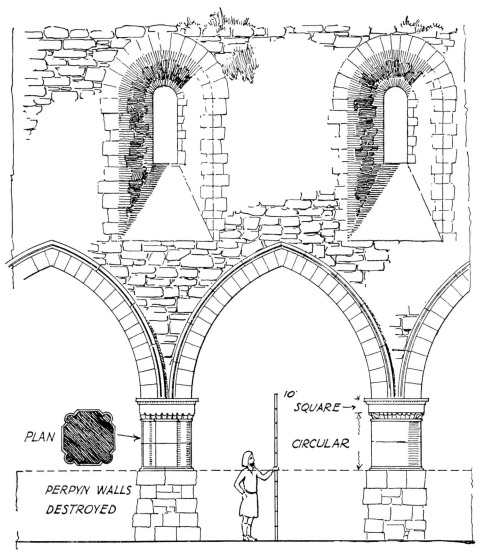

8. Jerpoint Abbey Church: nave arcade and clearstorey

removal of the S. aisle with an extension northwards of the cloister and the erection of a cloister arcade. All these changes, except the first, were works of the fifteenth century. (A curious and appar-

D

ently unique feature was a small structure—now marked only by foundations—projecting into the garth from the N. ambulatory. It was rebuilt further north after the removal of the S. aisle and *may* have housed a stairs to the rood loft.)

Another Cistercian church in which both earlier and later Transitional work remains is BOYLE (Roscommon), where the colony sent out to the neighbourhood by Mellifont in 1148 finally settled in 1161. The first building period, which must have begun soon after this date, is represented in the presbytery and transept with its chapels. In their walls are small, round-headed windows (9) and several rows of plain string-courses which once extended across the E. wall of the presbytery. There were doubtless similar windows, possibly two storeys of them, in this gable but in their place are three tall lancets of the early thirteenth century. Though the earlier windows are round-arched the presbytery and chapel arches are pointed, the openings are tall and the effect is one of stark grandeur (Pl. Ib). All the wrought work of these parts is in sandstone.

The church is one of the largest of the Order in Ireland, exceeded in length—and not greatly—only by those at Mellifont, Knockmoy, Graignamanagh and Dunbrody, all but the second of later date. It is also more complete than any of these and of commanding height, only the two last-named being more impressive in this respect. Unlike most of the other Cistercian churches Boyle had a low tower (later raised) over the crossing from the start. This was necessitated by the great height of the transept arches which rise above the level of the nave walls and could not have been covered by a continuation of the nave roof, as at Jerpoint and elsewhere, as Clapham[3] has pointed out. The extra east to west width of the western piers of the crossing indicates that the nave was not begun at the same time as the crossing or immediately upon its completion: these piers had to resist the thrust of the transept arches in the absence of the counter-thrust exerted by the nave arcades. The presbytery is vaulted as are the four chapels

Section of jamb ⅹ 3″
BOYLE ABBEY E. WINDOW: CHAPEL

9. Boyle Abbey: details

PLATE I

Ib. North Transept

BOYLE ABBEY

Ia. Interior of Church, looking East

PLATE II

IIb. Capital in Nave

BOYLE ABBEY

IIa. West Elevation of Church

which have chambers above them. Round arches span the transept openings and that under the west wall of the tower. The lofty crossing piers—square responds with shafts wrought on the angles and bold half-shafts central in each face—have squat moulded bases of small projection (10). Cubical capitals, some scalloped and delicately fluted, crown the crossing and chapel piers and both the arches and hood mouldings are square-edged.

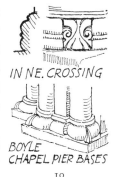

IN NE. CROSSING

BOYLE
CHAPEL PIER BASES

10

Building progressed slowly—the church was not consecrated until 1218—and there seems to have been not only a pause after the completion of transept and crossing but a change of designers; it is evident that the eastern responds of the arcade are in key with the work of the transept and crossing but not completely so with that of the nave arcades. Of these the five eastern bays belong to the later years of the twelfth century. The five round arches— in two plain chamfered orders—are carried by cylindrical pillars with octagonal capitals, scalloped, and make an impressive row (Pl. Ia) recalling, on a smaller scale, the nave arcades of Fountains Abbey in Yorkshire. The bases are simple torus moulds with boldly-carved leaf-spurs (11). Opposite, in the north arcade, the five corresponding arches also in two orders, are bluntly pointed in strange contrast to, but not greatly differing in date, apparently, from those on the S. side. A different designer may be inferred. The pillar plans vary: octagonal, and square with attached shafts. In the clearstorey above the arcades are small, round-headed windows. Latest (c. 1205-1218) are the three western bays and west wall. Round arches complete the impressive S. arcade; pointed arches, with a pointed arris roll, that on the north. The piers on both sides are square, chamfered on the angles, and the soffit order in each, also chamfered, is borne by engaged triple shafts (12). The centre shafts have a keel and all—together with similar corbel shafts, high in both walls, tapering down to a point— are crowned by interesting capitals of varied design but mostly of the same general outline (Pl. IIb, 13). In low relief, these capitals, and the triple shafts, are derived from the western English archi-

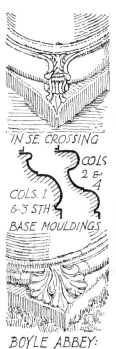

IN SE. CROSSING

COLS
2 &
4

COLS. 1
& 3 STH.

BASE MOULDINGS

BOYLE ABBEY:
BASES & SPURS

11

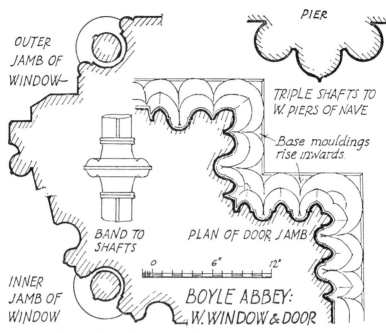

12. Boyle Abbey Church: mouldings of west window and door, etc.

BOYLE ABBEY
CAPITALS; EARLY
13TH CY., IN NAVE

13

tectural province: Wells and Llandaff cathedrals, particularly the
latter, supply many instances of shafts grouped in threes. Though
the English capitals are richer and bolder some abaci at Llandaff
are of the same section as those at Boyle. The small corbel capitals
on the aisle sides of the walls are of the same general design (Pl. IIb).
These capitals are influenced by the school of the Irish west; the
subject of the next chapter. Over the west door (Pl. IIa) of two
orders, strongly moulded, is a single tall lancet with a chevron
ornamented arch. It has free, filleted shafts, with many bands, to
its inner and outer jambs. On the inside these shafts are set
between pairs of small rolls, close-set and filleted (12) a small but
significant detail which occurs also in three churches in eastern
Ireland: Christ Church, Dublin; St. Mary's Church, New Ross;
and that of Graignamanagh abbey. The likeness of the whole
window to those surviving in the north aisle of the first-named is
remarkable.

One order of the processional doorway has been restored. It is round and the arch and jambs are of peculiar section in which the pointed moulding plays the principal part. The bases are very shallow. The claustral buildings were very extensive, rivalling those at Graignamanagh and Mellifont, but they have suffered ruin and change mainly through their use for military purposes in Elizabethan and later times. Still to be seen are the lower parts of the chapter house doorway and of another in the Dorter range, both works of the earliest period.

The abbey church of MONASTERNENAGH—also called Manister and Nenagh—(Limerick) of *c*. 1185-1205, though much ruined at its eastern end, still exhibits some features of the Transition. A pointed barrel-vault covered (it collapsed *c*. 1814) the short presbytery which had three pointed east windows. It had a western arch of two orders, also pointed, and its respond piers, as well as those of the transept openings and the nave arcade, have late Romanesque foliage-carved capitals to their engaged (14)

MONASTERNENAGH   KILMACDUAGH: O HEYNE'S CH.

14. Capitals from Monasternenagh Abbey Church and
O'Heyne's Church, Kilmacduagh

shafts. The capital of the south aisle respond is scalloped with crocket-like forms in the flutes. A change occurs W. from this point: the builders left the responds in position and built square piers touching the capitals, starting new arcades of four bays each, with pointed arches, very plain and severe. The walls west of the arcade are unpierced except for a doorway into the south aisle. High in the W. gable are two round-headed windows (15) framed

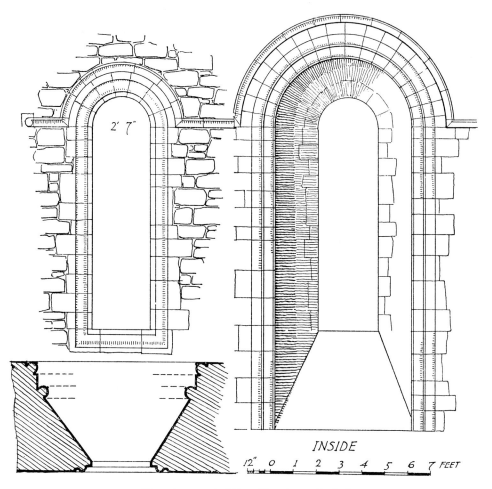

15. Monasternenagh Abbey Church: west windows

externally by a bold roll. Hollow-chamfered hood-mouldings tie the windows together both outside and inside where two orders of filleted rolls border the jambs and arches of the wide embrasures. Though the abbey is a daughter of Mellifont and was founded in

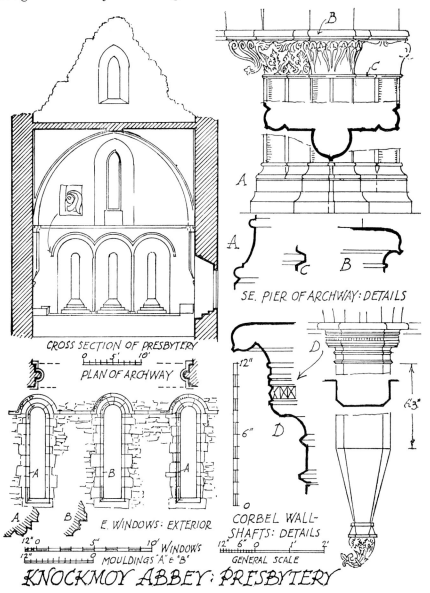

CROSS SECTION OF PRESBYTERY

PLAN OF ARCHWAY

SE. PIER OF ARCHWAY: DETAILS

E. WINDOWS: EXTERIOR

CORBEL WALL-SHAFTS: DETAILS

WINDOWS MOULDINGS "A" & "B"

GENERAL SCALE

KNOCKMOY ABBEY: PRESBYTERY

16

1148 all the remains are of later date. The church was large—nearly 190 feet long, with three chapels in each arm of the transept (115 feet over all) and the claustral buildings were extensive. They are now almost completely ruined. The chapter house projects eastwards from the dorter range. At some period, in the fifteenth century probably, the transept arms and the aisles were walled off and a wall built across the nave to the full height of the building.

Ruined Monasternenagh is—and must always have been—a gaunt looking structure, but hardly more so than is—and was—KNOCKMOY (Galway), built *c.* 1202-1216. More of the claustral buildings survive, however. The church is a little longer (203 feet) than Boyle and has two barrel-vaulted chapels to each arm of the transept. A pointed vault in two bays, with cross-, diagonal- and wall-ribs of square section, covers the presbytery. These ribs spring above a continuous, moulded string-course from long corbel-shafts with moulded capitals (16). The shafts taper and die into the wall-faces in leaf-carved terminals. Corbel wall-shafts are, as will be seen, features of the Irish western school.

Three round-headed windows, moulded all round outside and widely splayed inwards, and a larger pointed window over them, light the presbytery. The interior hood-moulds of the trio are plain; those outside are decorated (17). Each of the southern chapels retains its round-topped windows and to all the chapels there are pointed arches. In the wall between the south chapels there is a narrow doorway, an unusual feature in itself and unique in having a niche in its west jamb. The four pointed arches to the nave aisles are separated by rectangular piers broader than the archways. Curious capitals (18) with geometrical surface enrichment and, in two cases, carvings of heads at the angles, crown the piers and have moulded abaci. The few clearstorey windows are pointed and placed without regard to the arches below. The chapter house is covered by rough vaults on a wall and pillars, all of later date than the original work. It is lighted by five narrow, pointed windows of which the central three are of the early thir-

S.

6"
3"
0

CR.

N.

KNOCKMOY
E. WINDOW HOODS
17

teenth century and have bold chevroning to the inner embrasures reminiscent of the earlier work at Christ Church, Dublin. Externally the lights are moulded all round. The frater is large and had a pulpit in the south wall.

The sculptures which adorn the west wall of the " cathedral " of St. Declan at ARDMORE, Waterford, were described and illustrated in Volume I (pp. 164-5 and PL. XIX) because of their Romanesque character. There seems to be no doubt, however, that the sculptures and the building are coeval. The latter, though all its arches but one are round-headed, is of Transitional style and datable to *c.* 1200. In 1203, says Archdall, quoting from a source not now traceable, " Died Moel-ettrim O Duibhe-rathra, who, after he had erected the church, became the reverend bishop of Ardmore."[4] Since the details of the building accord well with the end of the century this statement of the learned antiquary, though unattested, is acceptable.

The church is of simple plan, a nave and chancel edifice, and embodies work of three periods; the first represented only by massive masonry in the lower parts of the north walls; the second, and most extensive, datable to *c.* 1200, and the third an eastward extension of the chancel. It is the second phase which has the greatest interest. To it belong the nave walls, except for the earlier work at the base of the north wall. All the narrow, round-headed window openings splay widely inwards to jambs and arches of Transitional section. The most elaborately treated window is that in the west gable above the sculptures. It has an inner arch, moulded, within that of the embrasure, borne by nook-shafts (now gone) with stiff-foliaged capitals. The four side windows lack this inner arch and shafts but the splays and arches are moulded as in the west window. Scalloped and foliage capitals to the vanished nook-shafts of the two orders of the north doorway survive. The internal treatment of the north and south walls is unusual; it consists of a series of very shallow panels, most of them with pointed heads but a few (to the west) with level heads. Above

KNOCKMOY ABB.
NAVE CAPITALS
18

these " arcades "—which doubtless framed wall paintings—there runs a chamfered string-course which rises over each window arch as a hood. On each exterior face a similar course does the same not only over the two windows but, purely ornamentally, at a point half-way between them where there is no window. In the archway to the short chancel are the most obviously Transitional features: the bold, half-round jamb pillars and the stiff foliage carving of the capitals. The strongly moulded pointed arch above them is less obviously of the period and may be later in date.

A structure which stands somewhat apart from other Irish work is the well-known octagonal lavabo of *c.* 1200 in the cloister

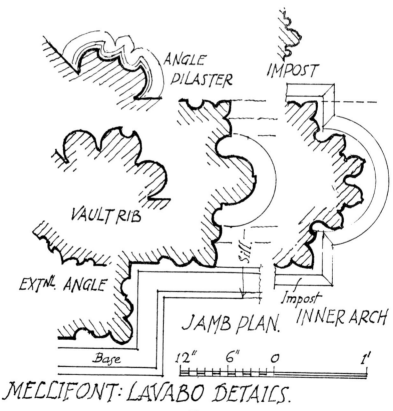

MELLIFONT: LAVABO DETAILS.

19

of Mellifont Abbey. It is also of the Transition, though its arches of three orders are round, their mouldings are decidedly Gothic (19). The hollows and rolls of the outer and inner orders are late Romanesque but the appearance of fillets and the keel mould at the arrises, and especially the undercutting of the group of filleted rolls which form the soffit arch, are Gothic. In one respect the lavabo has affinity with the western school: the mouldings of arches and jambs are carried across the sills also, thus framing the whole aperture. The string-course, which serves also as abacus, is a filleted roll, and the finely-carved, low-relief foliage of the capitals (Pl. III) has that classic flavour which is to be found in the work of the western school yet to be considered.

In this remarkable little building a stone basin stood on a pillar in the centre, as in some continental examples. Moulded ribs sprang from each inner corner of the structure, bearing a vault. Above this, in the upper storey of the octagon, there was probably the cistern.

Of the second church at MELLIFONT (3) there remain only the foundations and some low walls of a structure of the overall length of about 200 feet. Two-thirds of this length is taken up by the aisled nave. With the exception of the stumps of the two eastern piers, and some foundations, the arcades have gone but enough remains to show that there were eight bays. The most considerable survivals are the walls and piers—four to five feet in height—of the presbytery, transept and crossing. The first, which has salient buttresses to the side and end-walls, encloses, partly overlies and extends eastward of the narrower and shorter original work. It has the peculiar feature of an entrance midway in the north wall. In its south wall is a piscina niche which had a moulded arch and jambs of sandstone which had dog-tooth ornament as well as beaded chevrons. These are partly undercut and clasp a roll shallowly cusped. The fragments are Transitional in character and datable to *c.* 1200.

The north transept arm has east and west aisles, the former occupied by three chapels not separated by walls; the latter, which may have been vaulted, having chapels in the two north bays. There are piscinæ in the adjoining piers. All the piers are square. On the east side these are plain but on the west they have angle shafts and—in two cases—engaged shafts also, facing similar shafts in the aisle wall (evidences of aisle vaulting ?) The south pier and its respond have shafts to carry a soffit rib to the arch at the end of the north aisle of the nave. There is an important-looking north doorway; an unusual feature but to be found also at Inch and Grey abbeys (q.v.).

The piers of the crossing were reconstructed in the fourteenth or fifteenth century to support a tower, and the south transept was altered about the same period. So also were the nave and north aisle. Curious features are the pseudo crypt lately (1955) discovered below its west end and a small vaulted chamber outside the end wall. It communicates with the crypt which seems to have been necessitated by the fall of the ground westwards.

The cloister space measures about 135 feet from north to south and 100 feet across. There is some not quite conclusive evidence that the space was extended southwards from its original to its present dimensions. Short lengths of the base-wall of the arcade of the ambulatories survive or have been restored and on them are set some base blocks of the pillars. These blocks are set across the wall. Each has the shallow moulded bases of pairs of pillars, wrought in the solid. Some of these pillars have been found. They are short and carried capitals of the same dimensions as the base blocks but fluted and multi-scalloped. The arches, round and unmoulded, have been combined with pillars in a restoration of part of the arcade (Pl. XXVII). These remains are older than the lavabo and probably belong to the twelfth-century cloister. On the east the foundations of the Dorter range and much of its east wall remain, the latter within and touching the face of its predecessor of the twelfth century. Between this range and the Frater is

confused building, probably of late date; on the site of the Calefactory and east from it are the remains of a large, aisled apartment
possibly the infirmary. The remaining walls of the Frater are low
and featureless but the site of the pulpit is indicated by a thickening
of the wall at the south-west. Scanty foundations occupy the
kitchen site and that of the east wall of the cellar range. Of this
some massive but featureless fragments of the outer wall still stand.

Recent excavations (1954-5) have revealed the existence of a
passage or narrow court between the west walk and the cellar range,
extending the whole length from the south walk to the church.
Similar passages exist or have been disclosed at some English
abbeys—Buildwas, Pipewell and Kirkstall, for instance[5]—and
recognized as the route of the Sunday procession on its way back
to the church. At Dore and Stanley abbeys relatively wide courtyards have been found in the same position.[6]

Two other buildings of the later twelfth century also stand
somewhat apart, in their original form at least, from Irish architectural development up to *c.* 1200: the cathedral of CHRIST
CHURCH, DUBLIN, and St. Mary's Cathedral, LIMERICK.
The former, however, radiated some influences. A cathedral was
founded at Dublin in 1038 on land given by the Norse king Sitric
(Sigtryggr) "Silkbeard." Of this first building, which was aisled,
nothing remains. Under archbishop Lawrence O Toole about the
year 1162 the establishment became one of the Canons Regular of
St. Augustine and of the Congregation of Arrouaise founded near
Arras in the eleventh century. About ten or eleven years later the
new church was begun under an agreement between Lawrence and
the Anglo-Norman leaders: Richard de Clare ("Strongbow"),
Robert fitzStephen and Raymond le Gros. Of this building there
remain the transept and the adjoining arches of the aisled presbytery, which had a three-sided end with the aisle carried round it.
The eastern part of the vaulted crypt is also original. It has three
chapels to the east but there is some doubt as to whether these were
repeated east of the ambulatory above. (The nave is of the

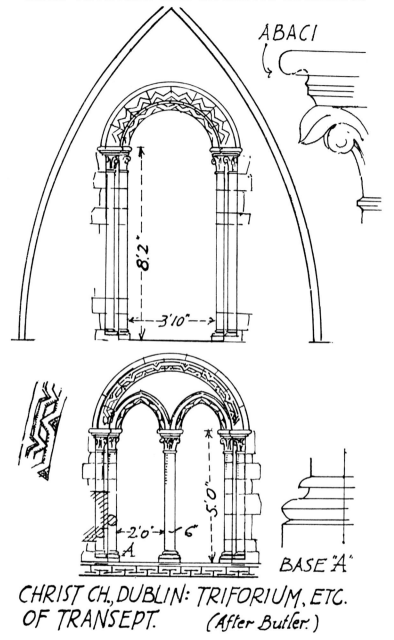

ABACI

8'2"

3'10"

5'0"

2'0" 6"

A

BASE "A"

CHRIST CH., DUBLIN: TRIFORIUM, ETC.
OF TRANSEPT.   (After Butler.)

20. Christ Church Cathedral, Dublin: triforium and
clearstorey of transept

thirteenth century and is noticed in a later chapter.) Allowing for a normal rate of progress—in rather abnormal times—the transept is datable to *c.* 1175-90. The whole structure has been much restored, indeed, reconstructed, but some features remain as they were over seven and a half centuries ago: the triforium arches, the south transept arm, and the inner parts of the clearstorey above them; the west arches of the choir and those between the transept and the choir aisles. In the triforium round arches (20), boldly chevroned, embrace a pair of similarly adorned pointed arches, and the slender marble shafts have foliage-carved capitals of western English style. The abaci are square in plan, boldly moulded and of a type common in the period in both France and England, while the foliage carving, ultimately derived from classic art, is also of the period. The clearstorey openings are single, sitting directly upon those of the triforium, and have chevroned, round arches in two orders carried by engaged, filleted shafts. In effect this single composition of triforium and clearstorey is enhanced by the wall-ribs of the later (thirteenth-century) vaulting over. Pointed arches, also in two orders, spanning the openings towards the aisle and choir have engaged shafts, triple or double, with vigorous capitals (Pl. IV) of figure, animal and foliage sculpture.

LIMERICK cathedral in its original form—aisleless choir, transept and aisled nave of Cistercian plan type (21)—is masked all round by chapels added in later medieval times, but the original walls remain substantially intact. The unadorned severity of this building may be due to Cistercian influence, indeed the curious feature, unique in Ireland, of arches across the aisles—their one-time presence indicated only by the scalloped capitals surviving here and there in the back of the aisle piers and in the aisle wall opposite—is an early Cistercian, Burgundian, system. In those early French churches, however, the aisle bays were vaulted on a north-south axis between these cross arches: at Limerick the latter bore only diaphragm walls, supporting the aisle roofs above. The short chancel has been slightly lengthened (in 1207 ?) and since

E

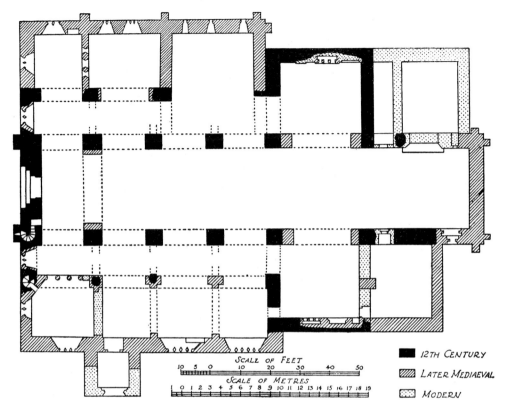

21. Limerick Cathedral: plan

altered out of recognition, but was almost square in plan like the transept. The nave arcade arches, four in number, are bluntly pointed and rise from massive square piers, which have corner shafts and are crowned by Transitional capitals. Above is the clearstorey filled with a row of round-topped windows sited over both piers and arches. There is a Romanesque west door, drastically restored in the nineteenth century, and a western tower raised on the west wall and on a high pointed arch transverse between the western piers of the nave. St. Mary's is the work of King Donal Mór O Brien and assignable to the years between 1172 and 1207

The major part, however, may be assigned to 1180 - c. 1195.[7] The ageing founder granted more property to the cathedral in 1192-4 and about the same time some of the lands of the dissolved see of Iniscathy (Scattery) came into its hands.

Of the once very important abbey of ST. MARY in DUBLIN only the chapter house and the adjoining passage or slype remain, embedded in modern buildings. Originally an Irish foundation, St. Mary's was a house of the Savigniac Order—a Benedictine offshoot—but it became Cistercian in 1147. The room, the floor of which is sunk some feet below the original cloister level (obviously to allow the dorter floor above to run level and unbroken) is vaulted in three bays. The groin and cross-ribs are of the same section as those in the same position at the abbey of Buildwas in Shropshire to which the rights of paternity were transferred in 1172 or 1174.

Of more austere architecture than either Limerick cathedral or the Dublin fragment is the abbey of FORE (Westmeath), founded by one of the de Lacys (probably Walter, son and successor of the redoubtable Hugh) for Benedictines about the end of the century. It was daughter-house to that of St. Taurin at Evreux in Normandy and because of this suffered as an alien priory whenever England was at war with France. Alteration and reduction in size resulted but the buildings are still extensive. Of no other Irish Benedictine house, indeed, are there any certain remains. The church, of c. 1200, could hardly be plainer; it is a simple rectangle. In the east gable are three large, round-headed windows, chamfered and rebated externally and with hollow chamfers to the angles of the inner splays. Equally simple are the remains of two north windows and a twin-arched piscina and ambry within and over which there are traces of colour: ashlar in paint.

Two Cistercian buildings, both in County Down, are datable to just before and after 1200 and belong to the last stage of the Transition in eastern Ireland. The earlier, INCH or Iniscourcy, was founded in 1187 by John de Courcy,[8] the Anglo-Norman conqueror of eastern Ulster, in expiation, it is said, for his destruction of the older (Benedictine) abbey of Erinagh in the same area. It was manned by a colony from Furness abbey. Only foundations mark the extent of the claustral buildings which were of the usual plan. Two extra-claustral buildings have been uncovered—a bakehouse and a barn ? The east part of the church still stands to full height. In the east wall are three pointed windows, simple but lofty (the central light is 23 feet high; the flanking lights just 2 feet lower) making a striking group internally where the splays of the wide embrasures meet in three-quarter-round shafts flanked by hollows. All the arches and the north and south jambs of the side splays have the pointed roll or bowtell moulding characteristic of

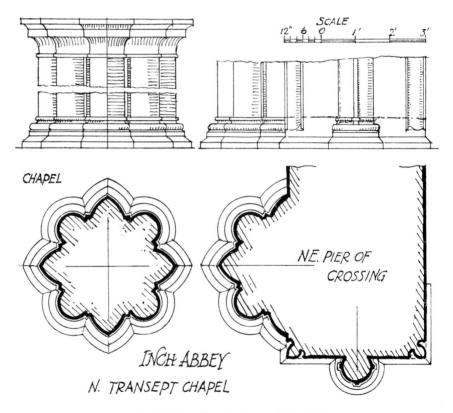

22.   Inch Abbey Church: transept chapel piers

PLATE III

IIIa.   Lavabo from South

IIIb and c.   Capitals in Lavabo

MELLIFONT ABBEY

Plate IV

IV.   CHRIST CHURCH CATHEDRAL, DUBLIN
Late Twelfth-century Capitals

the Transition. A three-light window filled the gable over. Pairs of lancets (17 feet high) in the north and south walls of the presbytery have the same mouldings as the east windows.

There were two vaulted chapels to each arm of the transept, not separated by solid walls in the usual way but having a pillar and responds of early clustered type (22), the pointed section alternating with half-round shafts. This column-plan type is regional, peculiar to the north of England (cf. Roche and Byland abbeys).

The crossing piers, L-shaped, and the nave arcade piers, rectangular, have engaged shafts to the east and west faces and filleted rolls at all angles (22). This very simple pillar-plan (only a plain rectangle could be simpler) is repeated elsewhere in Irish churches of the early thirteenth century (cf. the south transept of St. Patrick's Cathedral, Dublin, and the north transept, Mellifont). Such capitals as survive are of the simplest type: a bold cavetto with square abacus over it or, in the case of the chancel arch, with nail-head ornament under the abacus. There are remains of two main doorways in three orders. That into the north transept arm is apparently in its original place, but the other, now in the west wall of the reduced choir, was probably the processional doorway from the south aisle to the cloister.

The second building is GREY ABBEY, founded in 1193 by de Courcy's wife, Affreca, daughter of the king of Man. Its first monks came from Holm Cultram in Cumberland.[9] The church, small in relation to the extensive claustral buildings, differs from the Irish Cistercian norm in being aisleless and in having had a central belfry from the start. It has broad, shallow buttresses of early type, moulded on the angles, clasping the east and the north-west quoins. Two of the tower arches remain. They are of several unmoulded orders including a soffit rib carried by short shafts tapering to a point. In the east wall are two storeys of triplet windows with pointed heads (23) as in the church at Dunbrody abbey. The west doorway (Pl. V), a feature not common

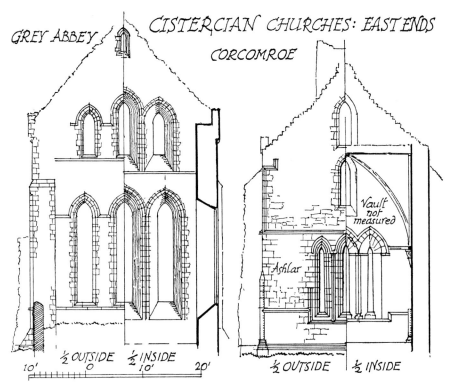

23.   Cistercian abbey churches: east ends, comparative. Grey and Corcomroe

in Irish Cistercian churches, has four orders of moulded arches, one with nailhead ornament, rising from engaged pillars. Datable by its details to *c.* 1220, and apparently not an insertion, this doorway may indicate that the church was not completed until then. There are two chapels in each arm of the transept and a winding stairs in the south wall led to the Dorter. A large chapter house projecting to the east from the Dorter range is divided by six pillars into three aisles. There is a slype and undercroft to the Dorter and, in the south range, a long Frater set at right angles to the axis of the church. It has a pointed triplet in the gable, west windows which are similar and a high-placed reader's pulpit in the same wall. Some foundations south-west of the cloister are evidently those of the Infirmary with its own small courtyard. The sewer and the site of the Dorter *necessarium* can be traced but the west range has vanished.

It is not surprising that the details of these two abbeys are in advance of other contemporary Irish work since both are directly English in origin[10]; de Courcy and his wife brought the monks straight across the narrow seas from northern Britain.

1. Clapham: *English Romanesque Architecture after the Conquest*, Oxford (1934), p. 77.

2. Thompson, Clapham and Leask: *Archæological Journal*, lxxxviii (1931), p. 15.

3. *ibid.*, p. 24.

4. Archdall: *Monasticon Hibernicum*, p. 684.

5. Thompson: *English Monasteries*, Camb. (1913), pp. 105-7.

6. *Trans. Bristol and Gloucester Archæological Society*, xxvii (1904), p. 33, and *Wiltshire Archæological and Natural History Society*, xxxv (1908), p. 541-81.

7. Clapham: *Archæological Journal, Memorial Supplement* to Vol. cvi (1952), p. 27, is of opinion that the original work may be of earlier date than any surviving Cistercian building in Ireland.

8. Thompson *et al.* : *Archæological Journal*, lxxxviii (1931), pp. 16-17.

9. *ibid.*, p. 17.

10. *ibid.*, p. 27. Also Commissioners of Public Works: *Seventy-sixth Annual Report*, for Grey Abbey.

PLATE V

V. GREY ABBEY
West Doorway

Chapter IV

TRANSITIONAL ARCHITECTURE: II

The School of the West

THE sub-title at the head of this chapter is here given to the architecture of a number of churches, datable in the first four decades of the thirteenth century, most of them erected in lands west of the Shannon. These buildings possess some features uncommon elsewhere in Ireland as well as sculpture in a consistent and distinctive style. Taken together, these factors justify the chosen title but the term " school " is to be interpreted as meaning a body of tradition, not as an indication of the existence of one guild of masons. Nor must it be taken to mean that the style grew up unaffected by outside influences—since some can be traced to eastern Ireland and places more remote—rather that it has distinct individuality. It might well be called a royal style since it came into being under the ægis of the kings of Thomond and of Connacht: Donal Mór O Brien and his son, Donat, of the former; Roderick and Cathal Crovderg, of Connacht. It is their architectural expression and marks the coming of an east and west cultural division.

The buildings are notable for finely-wrought and jointed masonry, generally of limestone, in the important features and also for foliage and other capitals carved in low relief in the earlier examples; bolder, even undercut but still compact, in those that are later. Arch rings, if not square-edged, are more boldly moulded than their supports and under-cutting of the chevron ornament (which survives to a quite late date) is common. Also common is the complete framing of window openings by mouldings noted already at Knockmoy abbey.

An early structure in which this feature appears is the roofless chancel of the small cathedral of St. Fachnan at KILFENORA (Clare). The east window has three round-topped lights, the central wider than its flankers, set in an embrasure splaying widely inwards which is round-arched but of less elevation than a semi-circle. Only a narrow impost moulding interrupts those of the arch which are carried down the jambs and horizontally across below the sill. Between the lights are narrow piers of triangular plan finishing in a slender shaft between mouldings. Each pier has a deep capital, one of scalloped form with little crockets in the intervals, the other carved with demi-figures of clerics. Each has a strongly-moulded abacus. This work at Kilfenora has been dated to c. 1170[1] but a later date for it—around 1200—seems to be more probable.

The cruciform, aisleless cathedral of St. Flannan at KILLA-LOE (Clare) is about 20 feet longer than Donal Mór's church at Limerick. The credit for the foundation of the church in 1182[2] has also been given to that great king, but the details of its architecture, aside from the presence of the pointed arch in all but one of its windows, belong to a phase of the Transition so advanced as to make a date in his reign rather unlikely. The seventeenth-century antiquary, Sir James Ware, the only source quoted for the 1182 dating, gives no supporting authority for it. On architectural grounds the earliest acceptable date is c. 1195, ten years after the Four Masters record the total burning of Killaloe, with its churches, by Donal himself pursuing a " scorched-earth " policy. It is worthy of note, as bearing on the date of the church, that between 1192 and 1195 the diocese was enlarged, and presumably enriched, by the accession of parts of the lands of the dissolved see of Iniscathy (Scattery) and the annexation of the whole of the see lands of Roscrea, also extinguished as a separate entity. The church (24) is the most English of the western group and here again it is to be

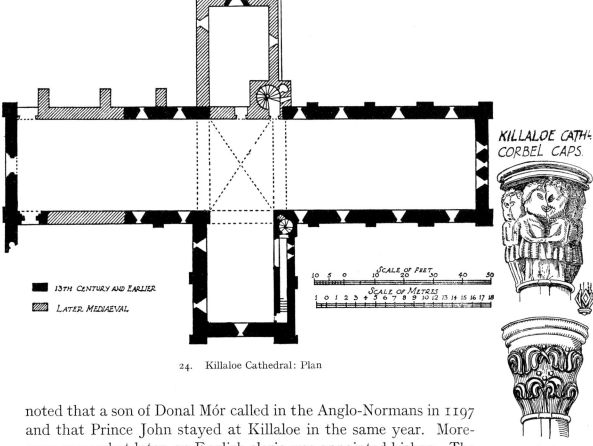

13TH CENTURY AND EARLIER

LATER MEDIAEVAL

SCALE OF FEET

SCALE OF METRES

KILLALOE CATH:
CORBEL CAPS.

24.   Killaloe Cathedral: Plan

noted that a son of Donal Mór called in the Anglo-Normans in 1197 and that Prince John stayed at Killaloe in the same year. Moreover, somewhat later, an English cleric was appointed bishop. The date of *c.* 1200, or soon thereafter, for the beginning of the building cannot be very wide of the mark; the western part of it belongs to *c.* 1225, the transept to a slightly earlier time. The mouldings about the large east window (27) show a combination and elaboration of those of the same features at Kilfenora. Both churches may well be successive works of the same master mason who—between jobs—may possibly have visited Christ Church in Dublin and embodied some new ideas from it in his own work at Killaloe.

25

26

The cruciform plan remains intact despite repair building of various dates such as the partial reconstruction, on the original lines, of the north arm of the transept, and its closing off and internal alteration. The transept and the belfry tower are almost central in the length of the church. Square buttresses clasp each angle of the east and west gables and the chancel has broad buttresses of small projection between the four narrow lancets in each of its side walls. Windows of this type, narrow, high and with acutely-pointed heads are found throughout the building. The interior presents a vista unbroken by any piers; the arches carrying the east, west and south walls of the tower die into the walls but have soffit ribs rising from corbel shafts. Here and elsewhere in the chancel, at cornice level, are a dozen such corbels: capitals of varied design crowning short shafts (25-26). In shape most are not unlike that of an inverted pear and bear decoration of that rather tight carving which is characteristic of the western school in its first stages. One capital has six "kilted" figures, holding hands and kissing; in others a reversed fleur-de-lis is found (26). The wall shafts, half or three-quarter colonettes, are filleted and terminate by tapering into knobs, knots, leafage, a horse, etc. There are very similar capitals in the south transept. The likeness of the Killaloe carvings to those at Corcomroe (Clare) and Inismaine (Mayo), as well as other places, is so close that the cathedral church may be regarded as their source of inspiration.

The most striking feature of the church (very difficult to photograph) is the great east window (27). It is bold and lofty; 36 feet high and 16 feet wide within. There are three lights, the central one round-headed and rising high above its fellows. The arch, jambs and sills of each, outside, have roll mouldings, a chamfer and the usual rebate and the trio are united by a hood-moulding following the outline of the arches. The well-splayed inner embrasure is spanned by a rear-arch of three orders, the first moulded, the second with curious, undercut "fish-bone" decoration (in effect, a discontinuous chevron with apices at the arris) and the innermost

Section c-d

Section a-b

c — d

a

b

Scale 0 1 2 3 4 5 10 15 ft.

27. Killaloe Cathedral: interior of east window

F

order has raised bars forming lozenge-shaped compartments. It is the piers between the lights that give the window its unique character; they are carried up from the sill splay for the full height to terminate at the soffit of the enclosing arch. Since the arch requires no intermediate support the piers are not functional yet the striking effect obtained justifies the means employed. Moulded jambs and double shafts with foliage-carved capitals carry the arch, and similar shafts and capitals adorn the intermediate piers. The jamb mouldings are carried horizontally, as a sill, thus framing the opening in the western way. (The central tower was raised by about 15 feet about the beginning of the nineteenth century—the time of Bishop Knox, 1794-1803.)

The Cistercian abbey of CORCOMROE—St. Maria de Petra Fertilis—well deserves its Latin name since it stands in the region of tabular limestone and richly green grass of northern Clare. Donal Mór O Brien is its reputed founder but, since its first colony of monks seems to have come from vanished Inislounaght (near Clonmel) in *c.* 1195, the prime mover may rather have been Donal's son, Donat. Its small, cruciform, aisled church, which has but one chapel to each shallow transept arm, accords well with a date in the following decade or two. The square presbytery has a ribbed vault in two bays (the cross-ribs have fish-bone decoration as at Killaloe; the others are moulded) lit by a trio of narrow, true lancets, with jamb shafts and hoods, below a single lancet (23). Curious pilasters, angular and short, occur between the lights and flank the group, and there are round shafts, with moulded bases, to the quoins of the east gable but only carried up a few feet. All this work is executed in fine-jointed limestone ashlar of remarkable perfection. The vaulting ribs spring from very short, tapering corbels. In the presbytery arch (Pl. VIa) there are two square-edged orders with a square hood-moulding. The stone-work is well wrought but the adjacent responds of the rough masonry transept arches, with their imposts, present a strange, jumbled appearance. It is otherwise with the piers and arches of the adjoining chapels, particularly that to the north (Pl. VIb); here the round columns burst into floral ornament below very slender imposts: dependent blue-bell blossoms on the left, inverted fleurs-de-lis on the right, well undercut in both cases.   On the arch of the outer order is a curious ornamental motive, for which a name, orange peel, has been suggested. It may be an elaboration of the scallops of the outer pillar in the twelfth century doorway in Killaloe cathedral or in a capital at Manister abbey (14a). The arches of the south chapel are plain and spring from capitals of which some have the low-relief, floral sprays to be seen at Killaloe; others of the capitals are human masks. West-wards from the transept arms which, with the chapels, were covered by pent roofs, there is a south aisle stopping about one bay's length from the west gable; two arches and the wall they are in seem to be reconstructed. It is not certain that a north aisle was ever built but it was certainly intended as the four built-up arches in the nave wall show. The closure may be a fifteenth-century work as is the cross wall with its mural stairs and small belfry midway in the nave. In the west gable are two tall lancets; the exterior (Pl. VIIa) is very plain.

TEMPLE RÍ or MELAGHLIN'S church at Clonmacnoise, Offaly, is a small edifice which has features of early Transitional, almost Romanesque, character: twin, round-headed east windows, each narrow, widely splayed internally and there framed by a pointed roll-moulding between angular fillets. Though without sculpture this church is included here in the western school because of its twin east windows. Though stylistically early, Temple Rí may, in fact, be so late as *c.* 1220.

It is otherwise with the elaborate and finely finished work to be seen in the remains of the great Augustinian house of St. Mary the Virgin at CONG (Galway). Little of the church proper (built *c.* 1226) remains but—rebuilt and inserted in its north wall—is a fine doorway undoubtedly of earlier date. Moreover, in the cloister face of the dorter range are doorways, exquisitely wrought in fine limestone, which also antedate the church. The details of these features, except for the lack of salience in the sculpture of the capitals which is characteristic of the western school, suggest influences from as far afield as France and a date relatively early in the Transition in western Ireland: between *c.* 1200 and 1220.

The north doorway to the church has five orders of pillar and arch. Originally pointed, the arch orders have been blunted at the

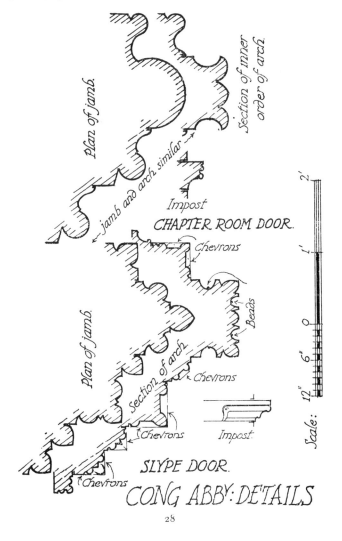

CONG ABBY. DETAILS

28

PLATE VI

VIb. Archway of North Chapel

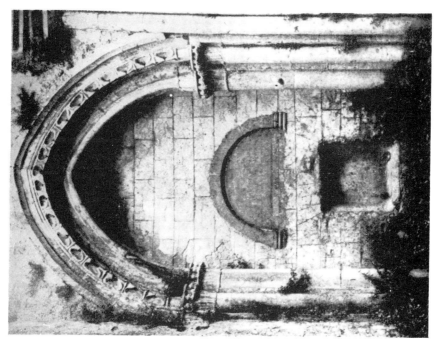

VIa. Chancel

CORCOMROE ABBEY CHURCH

PLATE VII

VIIa.   CORCOMROE ABBEY CHURCH
View from South-west

CONG ABBEY
VIIb.   Capitals of East Jamb of North Doorway

apex in re-erection.   Each ring has a bold roll hollowed on the soffit, giving a hook form section, and all rise from a moulded impost (Pls. VIIb, VIII) of rare profile but paralleled in northern France and south Britain.   As in the native Romanesque the capitals form a continuous, frieze-like block, covered with leafage ornament in very low relief.   This leafage is dervied ultimately and through many intermediate steps, from the Classical acanthus.[3] French-looking imposts, and very similar acanthus-derived ornaments appear in the chapter house and slype doorways and the arch mouldings (28) in both of these beautiful portals exhibit the pointed moulding, bold rolls, chevrons in variety, and lines of beading.   It is possible to believe in the presence at Cong, when this work was in hand, of some French sculptor or of someone who was well acquainted with French work.

Only two capitals of the much-restored (and—in restoration— too widely spread) cloister arcade are original.   One of these broad blocks supported by slab-form—dumb-bell plan—pillars set across the wall, shows a trellis-like decoration in low relief—(see also a capital in Abbey Knockmoy nave, 18).   The original arcade seems to be not much later in date than the doorways close by and may well be the prototype of the essentially similar design erected in abbeys and friaries throughout Ireland in succeeding centuries. Slender pillars in pairs appeared earlier at Mellifont (Pl. XXVII) but the slab type, with a connecting web as at Cong and specially suited to limestone, became the normal Irish form.

The western part of the nave of BOYLE abbey is of *c.* 1205-18 as already noted, and to the later part of the same period belong the numerous capitals (Pl. IIb, 13) and wall-shafts integral with the three west piers and inserted in the walls of the earlier work eastwards. All except the corbel-capitals set low in the spandrels between the arches of the older work rise from triple shafts.   The central shafts have a keel but not all have neckings to the capitals.   The same section of abacus (found also at Llandaff cathedral as already noted) is used throughout (13).   In plan most of the capitals are

EY. XIIITH CY.
XVIITH CY.
MODERN

SACY

CHAPTER
HOUSE

BOOKS
?

ROOFLESS NAVE

SCALE

10'   0   10   20   30   40   50'

29.   Ballintober Abbey, Co. Mayo

semi-octagonal but there are variations in form from a swelling inverted pear-shape to slender scalloping and nearly all bear low-relief, pseudo-acanthine foliage, cf. Cong. The exceptions have carvings of small human (13) and animal figures combined with foliage. The whole remarkable group, while distinguished from the rest of the school of the west by the forms of the capitals used, is undoubtedly related through its motives and carving technique with Corcomroe, Killaloe and Cong.

Not much later in date must be the large abbey church of the Augustinians at BALLINTOBER, Mayo, founded by the king of Connacht, Cathal Crovderg O Conor. It was Abbot Maelbrigdhe O Maicen who began and completed the church Tober Patraic, say the annalists who also note his death in 1221. In plan the church is of the Cistercian form but without aisles. Chapels and presbytery are vaulted, the latter with ribs rising from triple-membered wall-shafts (29) which taper through their whole length from capital to terminal of carved foliage. There are signs that it was intended to vault the crossing also. Round-headed windows, very like those at Knockmoy, persist (30). The three east windows are completely framed in mouldings—a recurrent feature of the western style—and small capitals with square abaci crown the outer shafts and two arches are chevroned. The capitals of the chapter house doorway echo those at Inishmaine (*post* p. 67) but Cong seems to have influenced the design of other doorways in the dorter range.

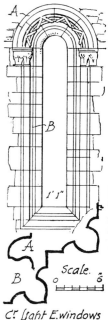

Cf. *light E.windows*
BALLINTOBER ABB.

30

The Augustinian nunnery at KILLONE (Clare) has a rect-angular church with a small cloister court south of it bordered by the remains of the three ranges. Sited on ground falling to east and south, there was opportunity—indeed, necessity—to provide an eastern crypt to the church. It is the east wall, with its two round-topped lights (31) splaying inwards to round, chevron-moulded arches and quite Gothic wall-shafts beneath the moulded impost, which is the main feature of interest. There is a passage in the wall, leading to the roof-walk, and its openings in the window splays

31. Killone Abbey Church: east windows

have trefoil-pointed heads. According to legend Killone is one of
the many works of king Donal Mór and datable to *c.* 1190, but the
work certainly belongs to a very late stage in the Transition, hardly
earlier—and quite possible later—than *c.* 1225.

There are several ancient structures of the early thirteenth
century which still exhibit the round arch in combination with
mouldings distinctly Transitional and sculpture of the western
type. Some of the churches have wings (not transepts or aisles)
attached, perhaps domestic in main purpose (cf. S. Saviour's Priory,
Glendalough, Vol. I, pp. 96-100). At one there is an incipient
claustral arrangement. All are situated in the O Conor kingdom,
distant from English influence and, indeed, from that of the
Cistercians, where the conservatism of the Irish masons continued
to express itself to a relatively late period.

The complete framing of window openings remarked upon in
the cases of those at Ballintober and Killaloe and the chapter
house at Knockmoy appears also in the pairs of east windows in

PLATE VIII

VIII. CONG ABBEY

Capitals, etc., of Slype Doorway, North Jamb

PLATE IX

IX.   DRUMACOO CHURCH, South Doorway

the churches of the small monasteries mentioned. Framing seems to be peculiar to the school of the west and to have its origin in the Romanesque (cf. Banagher church and Cahan abbey,[4] Aghowle church[5] and Killeshin and St. Peakan's churches[6]).

The paired east windows of Temple Rí, Clonmacnoise, have been noted already (p. 59) but their framing is confined to the

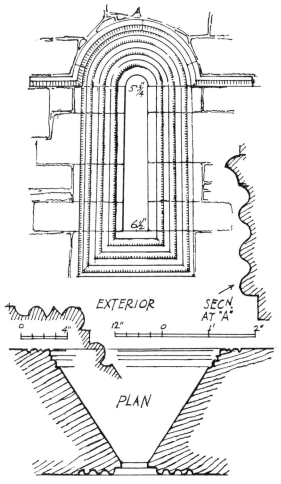

BANAGHER CH: WINDOW IN S. WALL

32

interior elevation. There are also cases of single lights, so framed externally, and—in some cases, internally also—which call for mention before the discussion of windows in pairs. In an apparently Romanesque window figured by Westropp[7] from KILFIN-AGHTA church (Clare) triple rolls on a receding plane surround the narrow opening which has inclined jambs. Much the same section of moulded frame, but in one plane with the wall face, encloses a window (32), also with inclined jambs, in the south wall of BANAGHER church (Derry). It has a hood-moulding with long lateral extensions and the effect is exceedingly archaic, the appearance strikingly like that of some fifth-sixth-century Syrian windows illustrated by de Vogue.[8] This likeness is misleading, however, since the coeval mouldings which border the inner embrasure are obviously Transitional (32): the angle roll is filleted and flanked by rolls and angular beads. At the east quoins were shafts, three-quarter round, the capitals of which survive. They are of late

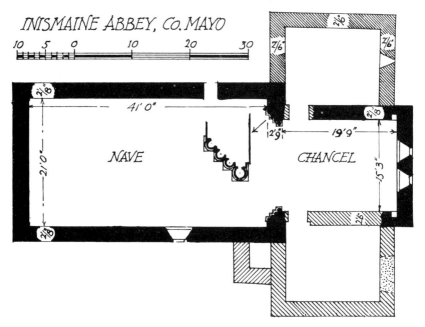

33. Inishmaine Abbey: plan

Romanesque type with low-relief foliage and animal carving. A date towards the end of the twelfth century—*c.* 1180—seems appropriate for the window and the capitals. Though Banagher is not precisely in the geographical area of the western school (i.e., west of the Shannon) it may be regarded as an outlier of the latter.

At another outlying monastic centre, DEVENISH (Fermanagh), less distant from western influences, there is a single round-headed window existing in the lower church. It also is framed in mouldings both within and without. These are distinctly Transitional and include one of a curious hook-form section (cf. Mellifont lavabo) (19).

One of the western group of small monasteries mentioned already is that of the Augustinians at INISHMAINE (Mayo) on the shore of Lough Mask and about fifteen miles from Ballintober. The church (33) is small, with a nave and chancel and north and south wings entered from the latter. Very little is known of the history of this " abbey "; it escapes annalistic mention except for the record of a burning in 1227 and the obit of a prior in 1223. He was Maelisa O Conor, and of royal blood, being a son of the Turlough who reigned as Ard Rí from 1118 to 1156. It is to this royal connexion that we may attribute, with reason, the erection of the extant church. The burning of 1227 need not necessarily have involved the destruction of the church, or of more than its roof, A date of *c.* 1210-20 would not be inappropriate for its most significant features: the east windows (34) and the pillars and capitals (35) of the chancel archway. The former, a pair, are round-topped. Each is framed on the outside in continuous rolls separated by a hollow, and the two are made into one composition by a hood-moulding with straight ends. A crude carving of a horseman above one end of the hood balances two grotesque beasts at the other; the actual ends terminate in simple leaf scrolls.

Similar mouldings, but with a keel to the main roll, enframe the inner embrasures unifying the pair. The chancel jambs (33) are made up of four slender engaged shafts, about three-quarter-round

34.   Inishmaine Abbey: east windows

35.   Inishmaine Abbey:
capitals to chancel arch piers

in plan, and have tall capitals, almost conical (35). Ornament of
stylized foliage and strange " combatant " animals in low relief,
cover the cap surfaces and recall that of the Killaloe capitals. The
imposts are of a delicate cavetto section but of the five plain arches
which rose from them few stones remain.

More elaborately treated are the pair of east windows (36),
also in finely wrought ashlar, of the church of Monaster Muinter
Heyne—O HEYNE'S church in the Kilmacduagh (Galway) group.
The lights are both narrower and taller than those at Inishmaine
and have a double recess or casement externally, flanked by shafts

KILMACDUAGH: O'HEYNE'S CH.
EAST WINDOW.

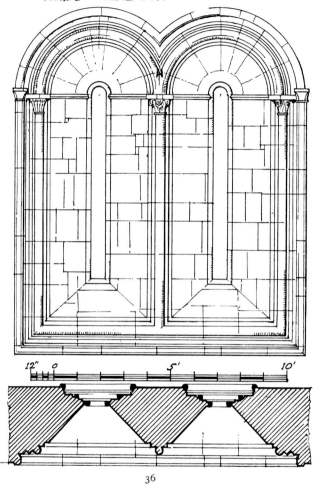

36

and having two roll mouldings. One of these, with a keel, forms the reveal of the light. The hood-mouldings are united by another in the shape of a pointed arch. Much more bold and original is the internal treatment. Here the principal rolls, slightly keeled, are really engaged shafts with capitals but have no bases where they

G

return horizontally: also returned are the square and chamfered side pilasters which finish in small capitals. On the splays a V-section mould marks the springing of the arches which have mouldings corresponding with those below them. At the east quoins are diagonally-set square pilasters (a survival from the Romanesque) with a keel section shaft. The jamb shafts of the chancel pillars (37) have fine fillets and their capitals are of lesser

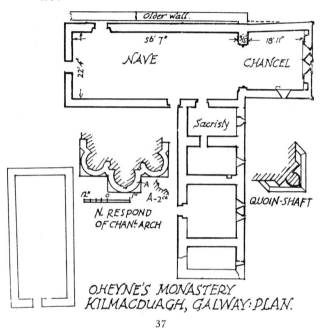

O.HEYNE'S MONASTERY
KILMACDUAGH, GALWAY·PLAN.

37

height than those at Inishmaine but project more and are more deeply cut. One of them is very like that at Monasternenagh; it is almost a copy (14b). The influence of Corcomroe, but ten miles distant, is evident in the chancel pillars and their bases. The vigorous quality of the limestone carving bespeaks considerable experience in working a rather intractable material and a late date for this work would seem probable. It is difficult, however, to believe the statement of the annalists that this is the abbey built on the site by Maurice Ileyan, bishop of the diocese, who died in 1285. Stylistically speaking, it is hard to accept a date later than *c.* 1250 for a structure so very Romanesque in character. Some time in the second quarter of the century, before the death, in 1253, of that vigorous warrior, Owen O Heyne, lord of the district and traditionally associated with the abbey, would be consistent with the architectural evidence. It may well be that Bishop Ileyan's work is only represented by the east range of buildings which borders the cloister-like enclosure south of the church. This range is definitely later than the church which also shows signs of alteration subsequent to its erection.

Closely resembling the Kilmacduagh windows are the pair in the chancel of the cathedral of CLONFERT, Galway. The external design—engaged shafts, with small capitals, flanking each framed light and carrying hood-mouldings—is the same. The uniting hood on the centre pier is of straight sided gable form, however, and has a blank roundel below it. The frame is a roll between hollows and the reveal itself is of strong half-round section (38). It is the internal design which differs most from that of the Kilmacduagh church; it is much more elaborate, indeed unique (Frontispiece). The wide splays have blank arcades shallowly recessed. Bold rolls (with a slight keel) form the frame and are, in turn, enclosed and separated by engaged shafts with carved capitals (finely scalloped to left and right, with stiff foliage in the centre) supporting the internal hood-moulding. The bases are shallow and stand on square base-blocks (with slightly carved panels) which are coterminous with a string-course. Both the workmanship and the material— a close-grained limestone—are of superb quality; most of the stones are large and the jointing is so fine as to be almost invisible. It is strange that this splendid feature has been regarded as either coeval with or earlier in date than the west portal of the building. Such early dating is untenable: the likeness to the Inishmaine and Kilmacduagh windows, both of the thirteenth century, is very close; moreover, the material, workmanship, sections of mouldings and design of capitals are similar in all three examples. It is more than

CLONFERT
E. WINDOW
Sec. A

38

probable, indeed, that the same masons who worked at Kilmacduagh also produced this, their finest work, at Clonfert. It rivals,
in the second quarter of the thirteenth century, the master-work
of their predecessors of some seventy years before: the western
doorway of the cathedral.

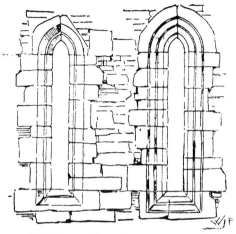

39. Inchcleraun, Templemore: east windows

Another example of a framed window (39) is in Temple More,
INCHCLERAUN, Lough Ree (Longford).

The last stage of the Transition in its western phase is exemplified in two County Galway buildings: the east gable of Tuam abbey
and the church at Drumacoo.

One of the Anglo-Norman Burkes who had gained power in
Connacht early in the century, founded at TUAM a monastery for
Premonstratensians. The east gable of the church (perhaps of
c. 1237) with its three pointed windows still stands. Each light
is acutely pointed and narrow but splays widely inwards in the
usual way. The arches are moulded—boldly to the side openings—
and have hood-mouldings with much-weathered stops. In the
broad hollow of the central arch moulding the chevron appears in
a peculiar form: lozenge-wise, suggesting a series of buckles. Deep

capitals crown the jambs; they are much damaged but it is still possible to discern foliage and small animal heads or masks upon them. Below the capitals the hollows of the moulded jambs still retain a few of the original slender detached shafts in short lengths between defaced band-courses.

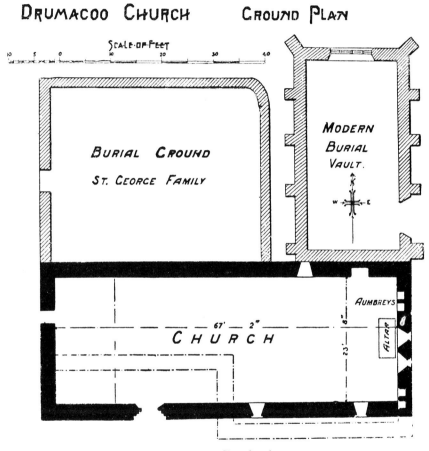

40.   Drumacoo Church: plan

In the church at DRUMACOO (Galway) at least three periods of building or rebuilding are to be seen (40). The first is represented by the north and west walls of a small church (about 15 feet wide) with a plain lintelled doorway of the usual type; the second is an extension eastwards (originally 28 feet wide) built in the early thirteenth century, while the third period is marked by the south wall. This extends for the full length of the church and has a short return to the north. The result is a rectangular structure about 67 feet long and of the uniform width of 23 feet 8 inches. The west

41. Drumacoo Church: inside elevation of east wall

door and the pair of east windows are eccentric as a result of the changes; the former to the north, the latter southwards. The two east windows, true lancets, narrow and acutely pointed (41), splay in to slender engaged shafts with stiff-leaved capitals and arch-moulds of the same section as the shafts. A horizontal string dips below the sill splays and the effect of the whole recalls Corcomroe. Twin ambreys with pointed heads flank the windows but one of the south pair is covered up by the end of the south wall. The south doorway (Pl. IX) of finely wrought limestone, claims closest attention. It is apparently coeval with the first extension and the east windows but was re-erected in the south wall when the latter was moved northwards. In this attractive portal all the inner features of the Tuam windows—with others added—are to be seen remarkably preserved: the buckle-like chevron lozenges (but with pyramidal spandrels) appear again in the second order of the arch, so do the slender jamb-shafts, set in deep hollows but the bands at mid-height retain their mouldings. The capitals (Pl. X), though somewhat damaged, also resemble in detail those of the jambs of the Tuam example. In variety of motives these capitals defy concise description. Foliage predominates; there are curious gar-land swags in two of them, a row of little animal masks (feline or dolphin-like ?) in another—reminiscent of the Romanesque. Some of the leafage echoes motives and treatment at Cong; the abacus moulding recalls the c. 1205-18 sections at Boyle abbey but is more highly developed. The masons or sculptors—probably the same who worked at Tuam—have broken away from the tight carving of the earlier period.

This elegant doorway is datable on stylistic grounds and the evidence of Tuam to the third or fourth decade of the century, perhaps c. 1235. In it the chevron, boldly undercut where it crosses the moulding of the first arch-order—which has a pointed edge roll—as well as in the lozenges of the second arch, makes a late (and probably its last) appearance, marking the end of the Transi-tion and of the school of the west. Two centuries later a second school, very largely western in its distribution, was to make its appearance.

1. Westropp: *Proceedings of the Royal Irish Academy*, Third Series, VI, No. 1, p. 137.

2. *ibid.*, p. 158.

3. Jackson: *Gothic Architecture in France, etc.*, Cambridge (1915), figures some capitals in Chalons-sur-Marne ambulatory and at St. Denis.

4. Leask: *Irish Churches*, Dundalk (1955), vol. I, p. 84, fig. 43.

5. *ibid.*, p. 84, fig. 44.

6. *ibid.*, p. 106, fig. 58.

7. *Proceedings of the Royal Irish Academy*, Third Series, VI, No. 1, Plate xi, 5.

8. *Syrie Centrale.*

Chapter V

IRISH GOTHIC TO A.D. 1250

I~~N~~ the period of the Transition the regular clergy and their patrons—native and foreign—led the way; the Anglo-Normans set the pace, however, in the thirteenth century, raising cathedrals abbeys and parish churches in the towns they founded and the lands they had brought under their sway. These lands, broadly speaking, included the whole of Leinster and great parts of Cork, Limerick, Kerry and Tipperary. But the Church and the monastic orders were not inactive in this building boom which the latter had begun; the Cistercians, for instance, built nine or ten of the abbeys which survive—several on the grand scale—in a Gothic which had shaken off nearly all traces of the Transition. The other orders were hardly less busy at building. But most of their works owe something to the greater cathedrals and ultimately, therefore, to the contemporary architectural arts of the west of England, as did the works of the preceding decades. It is not surprising that this should be so in the thirteenth century. It was from western Britain that the invaders had come; St. David's Head is but forty-five miles distant from Carnsore Point, and the western gate of Britain—the Bristol Channel—opens out towards the southern parts of Ireland.

Of pure Gothic buildings erected in Ireland by the Anglo-Normans the most important, if not the first, was the western arm (the nave and its aisles) of the cathedral of CHRIST CHURCH, Dublin, begun about 1212 and finished about 1235. Its design was inspired by the architecture of the English western school of Gothic; its wrought stones—of a Somersetshire oolite—were laid and sculptured by craftsmen and artists also brought from the same area.

Of the accidents which befell Christ Church the most disastrous was the fall of the nave vaulting, carrying with it the south wall, in 1562. It is not surprising, therefore, that the restoration of 1872-78 involved the rebuilding of about two-thirds of the structure. In this work the original details which had survived were followed with great care, however, and the spirit was in great measure retained. The south wall—replacing the crude erection of 1562— was rebuilt in its entirety to match the opposite wall. In this (Pl. XIa) the arcade pillars, perilously out of the vertical, were restored erect, in facsimile of the original, except for the addition of bands to the shafts of two western pillars. From the capital level upwards the north wall is unrestored but the vaulting is new.

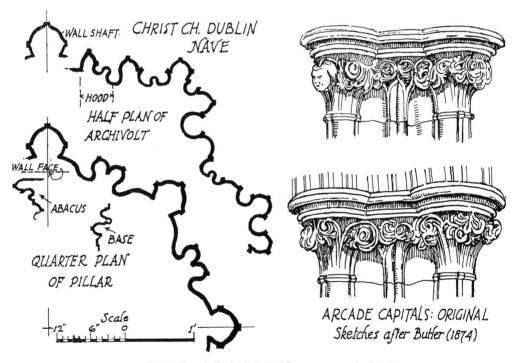

42.   Christ Church Cathedral, Dublin: nave arcade details

The arcade arches are in five not very clearly defined orders— three main and two subsidiary—in the full wall-thickness—a rich assemblage of deep hollows and rolls (some thrice-filleted) in the best thirteenth-century style. The pillars are relatively short and sturdy, a west of England characteristic, but quite original in plan (42)—a plan peculiar to Christ Church—made up of a nearly circular drum with eight attached three-quarter-round shafts (three times filleted), banded at mid-height, alternating with eight small rolls (also filleted) in pairs. The north and south shafts rise to the vaulting ribs of aisle and nave, the others to foliage-scroll capitals of the Wells school, with round abaci (42). Very rich in effect but not over-elaborated these pillars are unrivalled in Irish work.

In each bay the triforium and clearstorey are united vertically in a unique composition (43), with slender marble shafts rising through both storeys and enclosing a low arcade to the triforium, also marble shafted. The centre opening at each level is wider than the others and has a trefoil-pointed arch. (The similar composition at Pershore abbey church lacks the triforium arcade.) Unique also is the exterior design of the triplet, pointed, clearstorey windows: the centre window being flanked by smaller lights surmounted by steep gables in very low relief.

Despite their ties with the art of western Britain the masons produced in Dublin a work of great originality without any close parallel in their homeland. It may well be that this design owes its very elaboration to a spirit of competition with St. Patrick's, which was taking shape about the same time. It is as if the Augustinians— lacking space on the restricted city site for a church on the grand scale of its rival—determined to adorn their building in a more sumptuous fashion. In this they succeeded; no later Irish churches surpassed it in richness of detail. None the less, it influenced many of them.

That Dublin has two cathedrals of almost contemporary date is a circumstance which puzzles many. It has its origin in the unwillingness of the first Anglo-Norman archbishops to be beholden

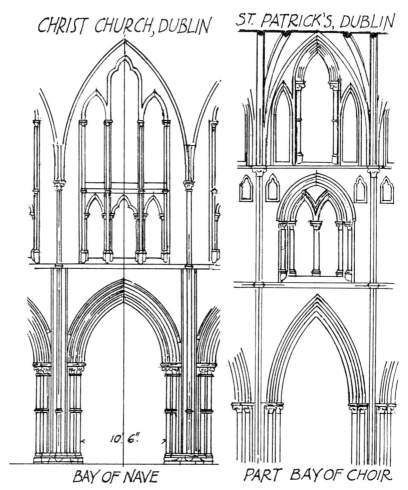

CHRIST CHURCH, DUBLIN

ST. PATRICK'S, DUBLIN

10' 6"

BAY OF NAVE

PART BAY OF CHOIR

43.   Christ Church and St. Patrick's Cathedrals, Dublin:
bays of arcades, triforia and clearstoreys

to the Augustinians of Christ Church which, because it was a
monastic establishment, was not altogether suitable as a metro-
politan cathedral. Moreover, it was an Irish foundation and had a
chapter largely Irish in composition and sympathies. There may
have been a lack of sympathy also in the inhabitants of the Norse-

PLATE X

Xa. Capitals, West Jamb

Xb. Capitals, East Jamb

DRUMACOO CHURCH
South Doorway

PLATE XI

XIb. DUNBRODY ABBEY

Interior of Church, looking East

XIa. CHRIST CHURCH CATHEDRAL, DUBLIN

North Arcade of Nave

Irish city with the newcomers, however highly placed the latter might be.

It is thought that these considerations led John Comyn, the first of the English archbishops, to set up in 1191 a collegiate church for secular canons on a site south of and outside the city walls in an open but low-lying place already connected with Ireland's patron saint. This church was raised to cathedral status in 1213. Of it nothing remains except, conceivably, some walls at the west end of the south aisle of the new church begun about 1220 by Archbishop Henry of London (Henri de Loundres). It appears to have been completed about 1254, the year of its consecration, except for the Lady Chapel, finished c. 1270.

ST. PATRICK'S, the largest Irish Cathedral Church, is 300 feet in overall length. It is of cruciform plan with aisles to both nave and choir, and east and west aisles to the transept. The Lady Chapel is of four bays and remarkably similar in plan to that at Salisbury in having aisles to the two western bays. (In this connexion it is worthy of note that Archbishop Henry was present at the consecration of the great English cathedral in 1225.) The choir is of four bays, the nave of eight. Each arm of the transept has three bays which are a little wider than those elsewhere in the building, an indication, perhaps, that the transept was not vaulted as both choir and nave originally were.

The church suffered much in the passage of time. The belfry tower (curiously placed at the north-west angle as at Augustinian Athassel) was in part blown down in 1316, the year in which the church was set on fire by the citizens to check Bruce's approach. In a serious fire which occurred in 1362 the tower and the north-west part of the nave were greatly damaged. Immediately after this disaster Archbishop Minot set about the rebuilding of the tower and the four western bays of the north aisle (see *post* pp. 136). The nave vaulting fell in 1544; the north transept and Lady Chapel became ruinous in the seventeenth and the following centuries. It would be tedious to record the dilapidations and repairs (often ineffectual) of the disastrous centuries; they can be studied else-where.[1] The later restorations are of more interest for the present purpose. Following a partial restoration of *c*. 1845, a much more thorough one was begun in 1864 at the cost and under the direction of the late Sir Benjamin Lee Guinness; later—in the early 1900's—the choir vault, which had been rebuilt in stone in 1681 and again in stucco in the early nineteenth century, was restored in stone to its present form. (It is of interest to record, in passing, that the cores of the ribs of the stucco vault were bundles of willow branches bent to the required curves.)

Though the authenticity of parts of the restored work is doubt-ful in some respects, the following sections of the structure are much as built between 1220 and 1254; the north and east walls of the choir (except for the external facings); the east wall and east aisle—with its vaulting—of the south transept and the three eastern bays of the north aisle of the nave. The restoration was drastic in character but it has left us with a church of austere beauty if less ornate than its rival. In the original restraint in the use of sculptured ornament simplicity in pier plan were combined with a fine sense of scale and proportion in a church which was to have a considerable influence on others to be built subsequently in Ireland.

The bay designs of the two Dublin cathedrals (43) are in strong contrast. At St. Patrick's there is in each triforium storey but a single arch (enclosing sub-arches) flanked, high up, by small trefoil-pointed niches; a design quite different from the unified triforium and clearstorey at Christ Church. One feature, however, in the former church—the single, central arch in the lowest storey of the eastern wall (Pl. XII)—may indicate Christ Church influence. It combines with three arches spread across the triforium storey and an arcade to the five subtly graduated lancets above to make a unique and serenely beautiful composition.

The simple and severe treatment of St. Patrick's Cathedral may have been due to a desire to build a large structure at a relatively low cost; the same may be said with regard to another abbey church of large size, at DUNBRODY (Wexford), but in its case the Cistercian rule of simplicity in building also affected the design, which is even more austere than that of the Dublin church. It is an early work. The foundation grant was made by Hervey de Montmorency about 1178 and a colony came from St. Mary's, Dublin, in 1182, but the building is of somewhat later date. The bishop of Leighlin, who had been a Cistercian monk and is credited with building the greater part of the abbey, was buried in the church in 1216 and a date of *c.* 1210 may, therefore, be inferred for the earlier parts of the work—for the eastern arm at least.

The church is (for Ireland) of grand dimensions—195 feet long and 34 feet wide, internally. Only the Graignamanagh and Mellifont abbey churches are longer. The transept, which has three chapels to each arm, measures 130 feet from north to south inside. There are five bays in the nave, which is some feet wider than that of St. Patrick's Cathedral. It is later by some decades than the presbytery and transept. The whole well-proportioned design (Pl. XIb) is severely simple.

There are three tall lancets in the presbytery's east wall, graduated in height and width. (The centre light is 24 feet high and 4 feet wide.) Above these are two smaller lights with round heads and, high in the gable, another such, still smaller. A pair of large lancets to the north and another pair to the west light the north transept. Round arches span the transept openings but are partially obscured by the pointed arches carrying the massive later (fifteenth-century) belfry tower. The eastern arch under the tower has taken the place of the original sanctuary arch.

Throughout the presbytery and transept the work is of the plainest: no more than a chamfer or single roll marks the angle of splay or jamb; a tapering corbel supports the plain chamfered soffit-rib of the arch to the south transept and the arches of the six chapels are pointed and unadorned. The nave has suffered greatly by the loss of the whole south arcade which fell in 1852 demolishing the aisle, but the north wall remains to its full height of over 40 ft.

H

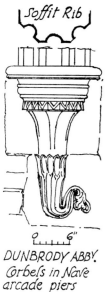

Soffit Rib

DUNBRODY ABBY.
Corbels in Nave
arcade piers
44

In it are five pointed arches borne by square piers chamfered at the angles. Each arch has—or had—soffit-ribs, some chamfered, others fully moulded (44) as are some of the main arches also, carried by moulded capitals as corbels, tapering downwards to finish in a bent, floral tail. The four clearstorey windows are each of two trefoil-pointed lights and are sited over the piers. Three have trefoiled rear-arches, dying into the splays, but the fourth (the second from the east and perhaps coinciding with the vanished pulpitum below) is more widely splayed to the interior where the twin, trefoiled, rear-arches are supported by jamb-shafts and a central pillar. In the west wall there were originally three lancets below multifoiled circles set in a casement above a doorway now built up. The surviving details of the nave, though still simple, are richer than any in the east parts of the church.

The cloister space was large (120 feet square). On its east side, beyond the sacristy and book store, is the chapter room in which two pillars supported a groined vault of six square bays. Next is a parlour or slype and the undercroft of the dorter. The latter was 145 feet in length. On the south side are the calefactory, frater and kitchen in the usual order: on the west no trace of the cellarium survives—possibly it was never built.

About the end of the twelfth century William, Earl of Pembroke and (from 1194) Marshal of England—the most competent administrator among the Anglo-Normans—set up his new town of *Nova Villa Pontis*, now New Ross. It was sited on the tidal Barrow, the main artery of his great fief of Leinster. He had married, in 1189, Isabel, the daughter of " Strongbow " by his wife, Eva, daughter of " Diarmaid of the Foreigners." Thus William Marshall the Elder, as we know him, became lord of Leinster. He divided his time between his earldom of Pembroke, his duties as Marshal of England and his Irish lands, spending some periods in the latter. The longest appears to have been the better part of four years from 1207 to 1210 and he was certainly in Ireland in 1213. He died in 1219 Isabel followed him to the grave a year later. Together they have

PLATE XII

XII. ST. PATRICK'S CATHEDRAL, DUBLIN

Choir, looking East

PLATE XIII

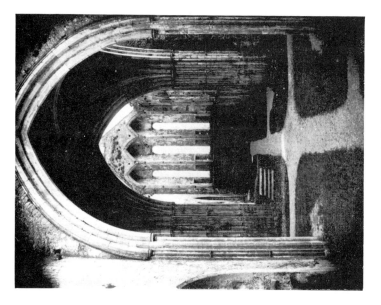

XIIIb. CASHEL CATHEDRAL
Transept, looking South

XIIIa. ST. MARY'S CHURCH, NEW ROSS
East Windows of Chancel

been credited with a strong and affectionate interest in NEW ROSS, and a cenotaph to Isabel—perhaps marking a heart-burial—recently found at St. Mary's church there is a proof of this interest.[2]

It is a reasonable inference that the church was begun by the Marshal and his wife and that the eastern arm at least may be assigned to *c.* 1210-20 and be, with the choirs of Dunbrody and Graignamanagh, the earliest Irish works in pure Gothic. The church was—for Ireland—of almost cathedral proportions. It was cruciform, some 155 feet in length and measuring 136 feet over the transept. In place of the nave, which apparently had aisles, there now stands a large, plain nineteenth-century edifice, but the walls of the choir and of the north and south arms of the transept remain to their full heights, though roofless. The modern church intrudes as far as the choir arch and thus separates choir from transepts. In the east wall of the former are three lancets graduated beautifully in height and width (Pl. XIIIa). The splays have banded shafts, flanked by hollows and rolls (45) and are spanned by moulded arches with a row of nail-head ornament. Small rolls in pairs recall (or precede ?) similar details in the piers of Christ Church nave and a doorway at Graignamanagh. The water-holding bases to the shafts have little projection and the slender capitals have very simple stiff foliage. There are similar lancets with the same trim in the other walls: a group of three near the west end of the south wall, a single light south of the altar and a pair in the north wall. In the transept gables there are also trios of lancets which have details varying slightly from those in the choir. While the north transept has four single lights to the east and two to the west, the south arm had a west aisle and has two chapels, conjoined, projecting eastwards. These are lighted by pairs of small lancets in the one embrasure. This, and an increasing use of a local stone (the stone first used came from a Bristol quarry) suggest that the south arm is later by some decades than the choir. St. Mary's was the most ambitious parish church of the early thirteenth century and it embodies in simplicity and grace much that was to be characteristic of later Irish structures.

Jamb Arch

Band

Base

E. WINDOW: CHOIR

S. TRANS^{T.} S. WINDOW

NEW ROSS WINDOWS

45

The building activities of the great Earl Marshal were not confined to his new town, bridge and church, however; he founded or endowed two abbeys for the Cistercians: Tintern Minor (Wexford) and GRAIGNAMANAGH (Kilkenny).   Since the surviving church building at Tintern belongs mainly to the later part of the century, consideration of it is deferred to another page (p. 121); Graignamanagh, almost certainly begun in the founder's lifetime, claims attention here.

About 1204 a body of monks from the abbey of Stanley in Wiltshire came to Ireland, at the invitation of a chieftain of Idrone, to found a new monastery.   After some exploratory wanderings and brief halts in various parts of Ossory they settled finally at Duiske, now Graignamanagh, beside the river Barrow.   The foundation charter made by the earl is datable, on internal evidence, to 1207 or soon thereafter.[3]

The church is cruciform, with aisles to the seven-bayed nave and three chapels to each arm of the transept.   It is identical in plan—and very nearly in dimensions—to that of Strata Florida abbey in Cardiganshire, which was partly completed by 1201.[4] Its total overall length is 212 feet and it measures nearly 120 feet over the transept.   It is thus the largest of the Irish Cistercian churches and with its claustral buildings (which surrounded a garth 120 feet square) the largest abbey of the Order in Ireland; a monument, now sadly broken, to the large ideas of William, the Earl Marshal.   Unfortunately, the extensive buildings are partly destroyed, and almost wholly embedded in modern structures.   The great church, too, has suffered much in the passage of the centuries by accident and from the hands of man.   The central tower, said to have been octagonal in plan, fell in 1774, carrying with it the vault of the crossing, its west piers, three of the supporting arches and the presbytery vaulting.   In 1813 the presbytery, transept and part of the nave were roofed to form a parish church.   In these operations the roof pitch and the gables were lowered and the building debris spread over the whole area to a depth of about five feet. Later the eastern sections of the nave walls were taken down and rebuilt and the nave wholly roofed.

It is known that John de St. John, the first English bishop of Ferns, who succeeded there in 1223 and died in 1243, was a constant benefactor and that the abbey received many gifts in the second quarter of the century. The assumed building period (1212 to 1240) thus coincides fairly closely with that of the nave of Christ Church, Dublin. Some of the details, sections of mouldings in particular, recall those of the Dublin church and bear the impress of a common origin in the western English school. The presbytery was vaulted in three bays with moulded cross-, wall- and groin-ribs, rising from thrice-filleted wall-shafts. There are banded shafts to the splays of the single lancet side windows. Of the three east windows the side-lights are round-headed, the central light pointed and the respective rear-arches trefoiled and trefoil-pointed. To the side splays were slender, free shafts set between small rolls and quirked hollows. The pair of lancets in the north gable have trefoil-pointed rear-arches. Two of the crossing piers still remain; their engaged shafts have unusually broad fillets and moulded capitals. The whole design of the presbytery accords well with the assumed date of construction and the trio of east windows may well be the fore-runners of those in St. Canice's at Kilkenny (Pl. XVIIIb). They have one outmoded feature, however: the round heads of the side-lights. The three west windows have the same peculiarity except that the rear-arches of the side-lights are semicircular, not trefoiled. Also round-headed are the twin clearstorey lights in the three west bays of the nave. Their rear-arches, also in pairs, are round and are supported by slender shafts in the centre and to the splays. As at Jerpoint and other Irish Cistercian churches, the clearstorey windows are sited over the arcade pillars. These are of square plan with chamfered angles but the arches are moulded with simply-carved leaves to serve as capitals. There are moulded soffit-ribs, springing from short shafts on corbels and crowned by capitals with both nail-head and foliage ornament. In the transept clearstorey are large, circular multi-cusped windows, those to the north now circular were doubtless originally cusped. A very elaborately decorated doorway (Pl. XIV and 46), round-headed—evidently also

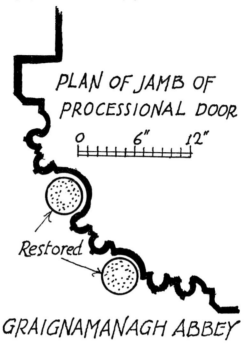

PLAN OF JAMB OF
PROCESSIONAL DOOR
0   6"   12"

Restored

GRAIGNAMANAGH ABBEY

46. Graignamanagh Abbey Church
Processional doorway details
(See Pl. XIV)

the processional door—remains in the wall of the south aisle. Its inner order is chamfered and multi-cusped and in the arch rings are lines of dog-tooth ornament and a most unusual minute, double chevron motive of similar dimensions and like effect. Pairs of filleted rolls between the free shafts of the jambs (46) recall the same detail at Christ Church and New Ross. The dorter range was about 168 feet in length, 22 feet longer than that at Dunbrody, and there projects from it a large room of later date: an enlarged chapter house and scriptorium in one ? On a north-south axis in the south range are the ruins of the large frater provided with an elevated pulpit recess near the south-west corner.

Very severe in its architecture is the cathedral of St. Brigid at KILDARE, built in the years following 1223, probably by Ralph of Bristol, who was made bishop of the see in the former year and died in 1232.[5] It is a cruciform, unaisled church which had a chapel projecting from each transept arm. The massive central tower— half of it a modern restoration—rises from square piers with corner as well as attached shafts, the latter carrying the soffit-ribs to the pointed arches above. All the windows are lancets, in threes in the gables, single or double elsewhere. The north transept, the chancel and the west wall are modern works on the old lines. Unique and attractive features of the design are the arches which spring from buttress to buttress, in advance of the side-walls (Pl. XVa). Above them are parapets of the stepped Irish type (pp. 134-5 *post*), now much restored but probably datable, in their original form to *c.* 1395 the year in which a Papal relaxation was given to those who visited Kildare and gave alms for the conservation of the church.[6] The interior treatment is very plain; the window splays are not moulded but the rear-arches, which are, spring from shafts with moulded capitals. These shafts are short and terminate in small, curved tails.

A good example of austere Irish Gothic, less severe in internal aspect than the church at Kildare, is St. Patrick's Cathedral at CASHEL (Tipperary). That royal, rock fortress of the ancient capital of Munster—palace and monastery for at least two centuries—was given to the Church, outright, in 1101. In it, in 1169, King Donal Mór founded a cathedral church between Teampull Cormaic and the Round Tower. This building gave place in the thirteenth century to another much more ambitious edifice, the work of three archbishops: Marianus O Brien (1224-1238), David MacKelly (1238-1252), and David MacCarwill or Carroll, who died in 1289; all of them Irishmen, vying with the Anglo-Normans.

It is a cruciform, aisleless building with a central tower. The eastern arm is wider than and of nearly twice the length of William

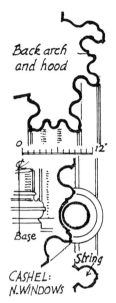

Back arch
and hood

Base

String

CASHEL:
N.WINDOWS

47. Cashel Cathedral
Mouldings of grouped
north windows of
choir

Marshall's choir at New Ross but of the same general character of design. There is no quite reliable documentary evidence for the precise datings of the structure; these have to be assumed from architectural evidence. Taking into consideration the likeness of the choir details to those of the New Ross work, and making allowance for the development and elaboration evident in them, a date in the third decade of the century—in the episcopate of Archbishop Marianus—is here assumed for this part of the church. The three conjoined side-windows of New Ross become five in the south wall at Cashel. In the north wall (Pl. XVI, 47) there is another group of five (originally six) similar lancets. These groups and perhaps those at Athassel, seem to be the earliest examples of the enfilades of more numerous lights to be found in many of the monastic churches erected in Ireland from about the mid-century onwards. In Cashel, however, there are associated features not found later or elsewhere: small quatre-foil windows sited over the piers between the grouped lights. Their inner embrasures have small free shafts between rolls and hollows, carrying the moulded, segmental arches. Also segmental are the inner sills of the openings. There were the usual three lancets on the east and also single lancets—one north of the altar, another in the south wall near its west end.

Westwards from the choir arch a change in the builders' intentions is obvious. It is marked not only by an increase in dimensions but by the use of the native, hard grey limestone for the wrought work and sculpture in place of the sandstone used in the choir trim. The symmetrical transept (147 feet overall and 31½ feet wide inside) is more than four feet wider than the choir. The nave, slightly narrower than the transept, is very short. It was apparently never completed to the full length intended; its western part is entirely occupied by the massive episcopal residential tower built by Archbishop O Hedian in the early 1400's. There can be little doubt that the nave was built during MacCarwill's long tenure of the see. It is more difficult to date the transept and crossing. The fact that in the south arm sandstone and limestone are mixed in the dressings may be evidence for a relatively early date. It is recorded that Archbishop MacKelly (who founded the Dominican friary in the town in 1243, a building in which the softer stone is used) was buried in 1252 in the Chapel of the Apostles.[7] Presumably this was one of the transept chapels in the cathedral. Hence it may be to him that the south arm of the transept is to be attributed. His successor incurred very heavy debts during the thirty-seven years he sat at Cashel. He founded Hore Abbey in the plain below the Rock in 1272[8] and the cost of this work, together with that of extensive building at the cathedral were, doubtless, contributory to his financial embarrassments. To him, therefore, may be attributed the nave, crossing and tower and, probably the north arm of the transept, at some date around 1270 before he had sunk too deeply into debt. In the gables of each arm of the transept are three lancets and in their west walls two or three, widely spaced. High over the north trio is a small rose-window, surrounded, externally, by a large blank, multifoiled circle of greater diameter. The rear-arches of the north lights are pointed but that in the centre is depressed to a segmental-pointed shape by the embrasure of the rose-window over. At the sill level of all the transept windows—marked by a moulded string-course—a mural passage, a sort of triforium, runs continuously round the whole. It connects with the winding stairs in the turrets north-west and south-west of the tower, and with the Round Tower, and it rises and descends over the choir arch. Extending westwards in the nave walls it joins the " castle " of O Hedian and the upper storey of the south porch, also his work. Two chapels project from the north transept arm and two more, much shallower, from its fellow. Pairs of lancets light the north chapels.

The low central tower is carried on the west by massive, many-shafted responds which are repeated, each slightly differing in detail, in the transept openings. The crossing is vaulted with chamfered groin-ribs. There are north and south entrance archways in the walls of the nave, intended to be centrally placed but actually close to its west end because of the intruding residential tower. Coeval with these arches is the vaulted south porch but its outer doorway is a fifteenth-century insertion. There is no north porch and that archway is built up. These openings have plain, chamfered arches in two orders with a soffit-rib (five orders in the wall thickness) as have those at the crossing. The capitals of the filleted, engaged shafts of the middle order are very typical of the Irish limestone style: with foliage scrolls as salient as in the English capitals of Christ Church but more compact—less deeply cut— conditioned, in fact, by the tougher material. One in the south archway (54) exhibits features found in other caps at Cashel and elsewhere: small faces amid the foliage with tiny hands clutching the stems. Throughout the building the normal hood-moulding stop is a human head, delicately carved (Pl. XVIIb).

All this wrought limestone work is well executed. It is well seen in the broad buttresses—with foiled, canopied and gabled niches in two storeys—clasping the transept quoins (Pl. XVIIa).

The most prominent feature of the exterior (excluding the tower-castle at the west end) is the central tower. It has been ascribed to the end of the fourteenth century[9]; a date which seems too late. Some such feature would be essential to interpose between the high nave and transept roofs and the lower roof of the choir (cf. Boyle, *ante* p. 32) in the absence of a gable wall over the choir arch. There is no sign of this or of a subsequent raising of the tower. It is true that the belfry windows are of the ogee-headed fourteenth-fifteenth century type but they may be insertions. The tower-roof was gabled to east and west within parapets. These are now featureless but may have been crenellated in the Irish fashion as were those crowning the other walls. No precise date has been ascertained for the appearance of the stepped battlement in Ireland but—in the case of Kildare cathedral—the end of the fourteenth century has been suggested already (*ante* p. 89). Their origin is also in doubt but at Cashel they are obviously additions—see the south-east angle of the choir. This great and relatively elaborate

PLATE XIV

XIV. GRAIGUENAMANAGH ABBEY CHURCH
Processional Doorway from South Aisle to Cloister

PLATE XV

XVb. ST. JOHN'S PRIORY CHURCH, KILKENNY

East Windows of Church

XVa. KILDARE CATHEDRAL

Exterior of Nave, South-west

church is worthy of the archiepiscopal see and its rock-site above the Munster plain.

The Friars Preachers, the Dominicans, arrived in Ireland about 1226, five years after St. Dominick's death and, in 1243, Archbishop MacKelly founded a house for them at Cashel, in the town, close below the Rock. The church is of the usual friars' type, a long rectangle without a structural division between choir and nave. To it, *c.* 1270, a large south wing with a west aisle was added. Still later some of the lancets—those in the east wall of the choir and the south wall of the wing—were replaced by traceried windows (*c.* 1450). There is a row of nine regularly-spaced lancets south of the choir, with plain dressings of sandstone. This row is, perhaps, the earliest example of the enfilades of piers and lights which were to become so popular later in the century. There was a trio of lancets of the same date in the east wall and another, limestone trimmed, in the south wall of the wing. Of the claustral buildings, which lay to the north, no trace remains. This is true of other friaries of the earlier part of the century but it is possible that there were no fully developed cloisters built at friaries in that period.

Another Dominican church of the 1240's survives at ATHENRY (Galway). It has been added to and altered in later periods but in the north wall of the choir there remain, intact, seven lancets, closely grouped, which are original. Since the most distinctive features of the buildings are of the fourteenth century further discussion of it belongs to a later chapter (*post* pp. 126-8).

The Dominicans of Cashel and Athenry seem to have been better endowed than the Friars Minor who arrived in Ireland in 1232; the brethren of St. Francis had struggling communities at KILKENNY and elsewhere in receipt of royal alms at this period. This was certainly so at Kilkenny where they were given grants by the king while erecting their church about 1245 and later. The foundation date is before 1245 but, as often happened, the permanent buildings were not undertaken at once; doubtless funds had to be accumulated. What remains of the original church is simpler and much less windowed than either Cashel or Athenry. The great east window at Kilkenny belongs to the next century and the following chapter.

Two other houses of the Friars Minor: CASTLEDERMOT (Kildare) and WATERFORD (now known as the French Church) were also receiving royal alms about 1247.[10] Even the foundation dates are in doubt; the precise dating of the original work surviving in the ruined churches is not possible but some time in the 1240's is most probable for both. This work is unadorned, even poverty-stricken. There are single lancets, widely-spaced but not much splayed, in the north wall and a pair in the west wall of the Castle-dermot church, and at Waterford a trio in the east wall. Both churches were much altered in later times; the former by a length-ening of the choir and the addition of a large north wing to the nave (*post* p. 125) and the latter by a similar addition to the south of the nave.

Equally imprecise are the foundation and building dates of CLAREGALWAY friary. The most often quoted date, 1290,[11] is not compatible with the presence of fairly widely-spaced lancets—six, originally seven—north and south of the choir, and the south-wards position of the cloister, as at Castledermot, Kilkenny and Nenagh. These suggest a date of *c.* 1240. Moreover, the friary is mentioned in an important list of 1260.[12] Short lancets overlook the cloister, and there were three in the east wall where a large tracery window now stands. Like the others Claregalway was altered and added to in later times (*post* p. 130). Its domestic buildings are of later date than the church but lie to the south, as was usual in the earlier Franciscan establishments.

In comparison with the struggling Franciscan communities of the first half of the thirteenth century the Canons Regular seem to have been wealthy in that period. This was doubtless because they had the patronage of powerful Anglo-Norman lords who endowed their Order liberally with supporting lands. The friars had chosen town sites for their first houses; the canons, rural places where there was ample room for extensive claustral and other buildings. One

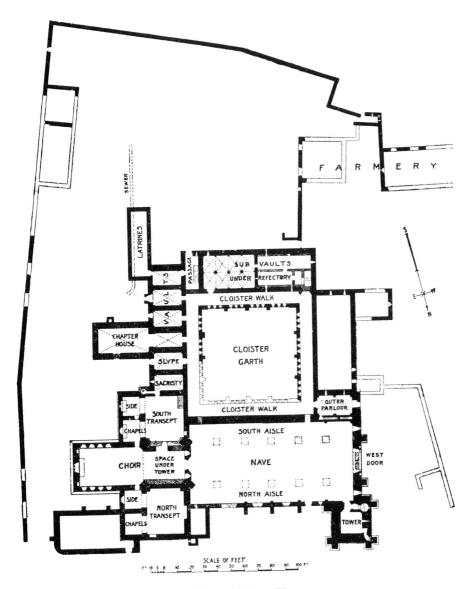

48. Athassel Priory: Plan

I

such site was that of ATHASSEL (Tipperary) on the right bank of the river Suir, south of Golden. Here there still stand the remains of one of the most extensive monasteries (48) ever to be built in Ireland. Its courts cover nearly four acres. Roofless and shattered as it is to-day it is in extent the most impressive of the achievements of the Augustinians. Of the precise foundation date of the priory there is no record but the founder is said to have been William de Burgh, the first of the Burkes, who came to Ireland in 1177. After a career of conquest (remembered by the annalists as ruthless and ferocious) he died in 1205 and is said to have been buried in the priory.[13] There is no doubt about the patronage of the later Burkes: William's son, Walter (*ob.* 1208) and his grandson, Richard (*ob.* 1326), certainly, were buried in the priory church.

The church, dedicated to St. Edmund, King and Martyr, is cruciform and nearly 210 feet in internal length. It had aisles, apparently vaulted, to the nave and a massive belfry tower, now broken down, at the north-west corner. To each arm of the transept there were two chapels and, on the north-east, another larger one of later date. But very precise dating is not attainable; at least four periods are discernible. Of these the earliest is the eastern arm; to the latest belong alterations and reduction in size during the fifteenth century. The works of the periods between are not easy to disentangle and define in extent. Opposite each other in the side-walls of the choir are groups of five lancets, close-set and regularly spaced. They are quite plainly treated internally in contrast to the groups in Cashel cathedral (p. 90) but remarkably similar to the row of nine in St. Dominick's church there (p. 93) which was founded in 1243. The Athassel windows may well be the forerunners of those in the Cashel friary church and be, perhaps, works of the third decade of the century. Over the crossing there was apparently a tower from the first, borne by four arches of which only one—that to the south transept—still stands. Its several chamfered orders spring from half-trefoil plan pillar responds based high upon the top of an original screen wall to the transept. The destroyed north archway was similar but both screen walls are now obscured by thick walls inserted to support a tower of the fifteenth century, erected in place of the original. It is on record that in 1447 " certain nobles " devastated and burned the greater part of the priory[14] and the later tower must be subsequent in date to this outrage. That the nave was left roofless from this date is shown by the absence of any roof creasing in the west face of the tower. The arcades of six bays have disappeared from the nave but some wall-shafts remain in the north aisle wall. From these and the surviving details of the large west window (flanked by small trefoil-pointed niches) and of the salient buttresses, a date in the third quarter of the century—or even later—may be inferred. In this connexion it is to be noted that the patron, William de Burgh, Earl of Ulster, was active and powerful at this time. He died in 1280 and, it is said, was buried at Athassel.

Striking and, as to date, rather puzzling features are the fine doorway (49) and the arched recess above it, both flanked by trefoil-pointed niches or windows, in the wall which divides the nave from the choir. The doorway is in four orders. Its splayed jambs had detached shafts of which the foliage capitals and water-holding bases survive. Each arch order has three rolls, the arris-roll filleted, and there is dog-tooth or nail-head ornament to the outer and third orders. Over the doorway is a wide but shallow arched recess crowned by a hood-moulding in gable form. It was, perhaps, originally open and held the great Crucifix—the Rood—and attendant statues, but was built up when, in the fifteenth century, the tower was raised upon the dividing wall. On the evidence of their details these two features appear to be later than the choir and earlier than the nave; a date c. 1260 seems appropriate. Preserved at the priory are fragments of vigorous carving, capitals and the like—possibly from the crossing—which recall the Christ Church style. Leading to the first floor refectory is a fine doorway in three orders, with filleted engaged shafts, foliage capitals and arch moulds very similar to those of the choir entrance

— ELEVATION —

Scale [ ] of Feet

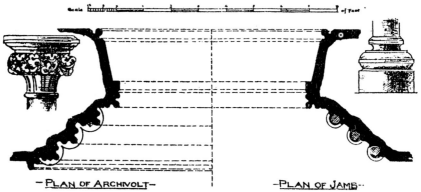

— PLAN OF ARCHIVOLT —   — PLAN OF JAMB —

49. Athassel Abbey Church: west doorway of choir

and doubtless of the same date. Also among the fragments are capitals with little peering heads like those at nearby Cashel but less competent in execution.

Surrounding a space of about 90 feet square are the claustral ranges; the dorter over 90 feet in length, vaulted in the lower storey, with a chapter house jutting from it and a long *necessarium*; a refectory above sub-vaults and a cellar wing on the west with an outer parlour. There are extra-claustral buildings, among them a vaulted gate-house. The ambulatory walls belong to the latest period of building and will be dealt with later.

At the close of the twelfth century Geoffrey de Montemarisco, one of the prominent Anglo-Normans, founded a priory for Augustinian Canons at KELLS (Kilkenny). The surviving buildings, very ruinous, are of various and, in parts, indeterminable but certainly later date. Their precincts are two courtyards within many-towered walls and cover five acres: the most extensive monastic enclosure in Ireland. In the ruined church—originally a cruciform structure with a Lady Chapel to the north-east, and the stump of a belfry tower at the north-west angle (as at Athassel)— no recognizably early feature remains. The towers, one attached to the south wall of the choir, another beside the inner gateway and four more to the walls of the large outer court, are domestic in purpose and of the tower-house type characteristic of the fifteenth century. Most of the claustral buildings are levelled but it is clear that there was an upper-storey frater—in which twin lancets survive—and a kitchen external to the cloister, as was usual in Canons' houses. Part of a central tower still stands in the church but the shallow transept has vanished, save for foundations. The north transept had a western aisle and the nave an aisle to the north.

The thirteenth-century cathedral at FERNS (Wexford), apparently, was intended to be on the same scale as that completed later at Kilkenny and was very similar in plan in having—in addition to an aisled nave, a transept and central tower—a long

presbytery with aisles for nearly half its length.[15] Of the original
work only the presbytery remains, but without its aisles. That it
was the intention of the first or some later builders to have an even
larger structure has been discovered recently (1956) in excavation
east of the presbytery. Here, at a distance of about 55 feet, there
was found the foundation of a massive east wall: either an aban-
doned original scheme or for a later extension which, in its turn,
was not proceeded with. The church was in all probability the work
of John St. John, the first English bishop of the see, between 1223
and 1243. It was burnt in 1577 and is described, eleven years later,
as " being in ruin and great decaie." At the end of the eighteenth
century only the belfry, traces of the transept and the presbytery
remained.   The latter, with some buildings of 1817, is the cathedral
of the Protestant diocese. In the east wall there are two lancets
(on each side of a later window, restored), two vescia-shaped
windows in the gable over and pairs of lancets in the side-walls
near the east end. Also still in position are the pillared east and
west responds of the arcades—originally three-arched—to the side
aisles. Incomplete and greatly injured but of greater architectural
interest is the detached structure of about the same date standing
some 75 feet east of the presbytery gable, axial with it and of
the same overall width. Its floor level, however, is about 4 feet
below that of the cathedral. The east and west walls are gone but
low and broad buttresses clasping the angles of the former and
foundations extending about 18 feet westwards remain. It now
presents two walls over 23 feet apart, each originally filled by seven
evenly spaced lancets. Only five of these in the north wall and one
on the south side remain complete. They rise from a continuous
moulded string-course. The hood-mould is also continuous and a
bold corbel-table crowns one wall. The piers rise from an inner
string and bevel inwards to twice-banded shafts (all of them now
gone) with bases and foliage capitals bearing moulded arches with
a row of dog-tooth ornament. These *enfilades* of pier and arch,
most striking when complete, are the logical development of the

PLATE XVI

XVI. CASHEL CATHEDRAL

North Windows of Choir

PLATE XVII

XVIIa.   Exterior View from South-west

XVIIb.   Capitals in Transept

CASHEL CATHEDRAL

grouping of side windows begun at New Ross (p. 85) and carried further at Cashel cathedral (Pl. XVI). Numerous lancets closely grouped—like the nine in the Dominican church at Cashel of *c.* 1243—were to become common in later monastic churches but in none of these do the windows completely fill *both* walls as in this structure.

The purpose of this unusual building is an enigma. It was certainly not part of the cathedral, as has been supposed; Sir Alfred Clapham's study makes this clear.[15] There are several possibilities, none of them fully satisfying. One is that it was a parish church; another that it may have been a choir for the Augustinians of the " abbey " to the south (rebuilt by King Dermot in 1160) the church of which may have been thought insufficiently important in *c.* 1240; a third surmise is that it was a chapel enclosing the tomb of the original founder of the see, St. Aidan or Maidoc. In support of the second possibility is the fact that ample lighting from high-set windows was favoured by the Regular Canons in their choirs (cf. Athassel). One envisages, as a matter of course (both here and at Athassel) rows of canons' stalls with backs reaching to the string-course.

1. Bernard: *Cathedral Church of St. Patrick, Dublin,* London (1903); Monck Mason: *History* of the same; numerous other works, guides, etc.

2. Leask: *Journal of Royal Society of Antiquaries, Dublin,* Vol. 78, pp. 65-9.

3. Bernard and Butler: " Charters of Duiske Abbey," *Proceedings of the Royal Irish Academy,* 35, C.1 (1918-20), pp. 14-19.

4. Radford: *Ancient and Historical Buildings Guide* to Strata Florida Abbey, H.M.S.O., London (1941).

5. Ware-Harris (Works of Sir James Ware): I, p. 385.

6. *Calendar of Papal Letters,* IV, p. 507.

7. Ware-Harris, I, p. 472.

8. Thompson *et al.* : *Archæological Journal,* lxxxviii (1931), p. 30.

9. Commissioners of Public Works: *Seventy-sixth Annual Report* (1907-1908), p. 6.

10. *Calendar of Documents relating to Ireland* (C.D.I.), London (1875-86), I, p. 429.

11. Ware-Harris, I, p. 506; Archdall: *Monasticon Hibernicum,* p. 640; Lodge: *Peerage* App.

12. *Calendar of Papal Letters,* X, p. 344.

13. Clapham: *Archæological Journal, Memorial Supplement* to cvi (1952), pp. 36-9.

14. *ibid.,* Pl. vii A, drawing of 1786 by Austin Cooper.

15. *ibid.,* pp. 36-9.

Chapter VI

IRISH GOTHIC
IN THE LATER THIRTEENTH CENTURY

THE preceding chapter was devoted to buildings erected in the
earlier decades of the thirteenth century; in this chapter those of
the succeeding fifty years will be considered. The study of some
of the earlier structures—Cashel cathedral and Athassel priory, for
example, which were not completed before the mid-century—has
already been carried, for convenience, beyond that date. The year
1250 is not marked by any notable change in architectural fashion
but it is the beginning of a period in which church and monastic
building activity accelerated markedly. The tide of Anglo-Norman
power was rising; everywhere in the areas more or less subject to
that rule the builders of castle, church and monastery were busy.
In Dublin the two cathedrals were complete, or nearly so; at Cashel
St. Patrick's Cathedral on the Rock was progressing but the 1250's
and 1260's were to see the start of at least three other cathedrals,
eight or more friaries and several churches of some architectural
importance. A special factor in this speeding up was the patronage
of the leading Anglo-Norman nobles, but hardly less so was the zeal
of the episcopate increasingly manned by English bishops. John
Comyn and Henry of London had made their mark in Dublin, and
John de St. John at Ferns; at KILKENNY bishops Hugh de
Mapilton and Geffrey St. Leger were to complete a very important
work, the cathedral of St. Canice, in the second half of the century.

Bishop Hugh (1251-56) is said " to have put the first hand to it,
and at his own proper labour and cost nearly brought the pile to

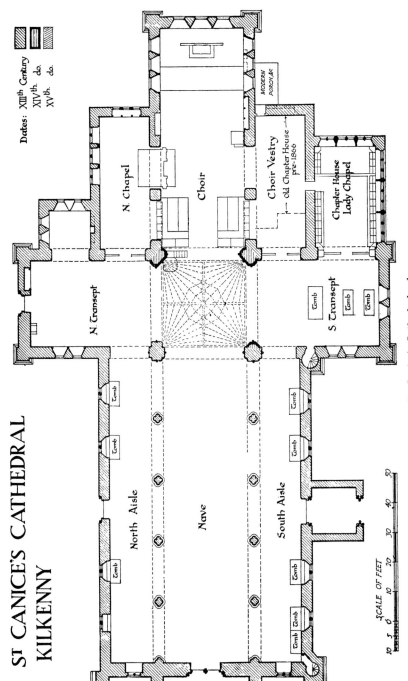

ST CANICE'S CATHEDRAL
KILKENNY

Dates: XIIIth Century
XIVth. do.
XVth. do.

N. Chapel

Choir

Choir Vestry

Old Chapter House pre-1866

MODERN PORCH

Chapter House
Lady Chapel

N. Transept

S. Transept

Tomb

Tomb
Tomb

North Aisle

Nave

South Aisle

Tomb

Tomb

Tomb

Tomb

Tomb
Tomb

SCALE OF FEET

10 5 0   10   20   30   40   50

50.   St. Canice's Cathedral: plan

completion."[1] Explicit as is this statement there is difficulty in believing that the cathedral was begun and nearly completed in five years. To Hugh should be given the greatest measure of credit, perhaps, but some may also be assigned to predecessors who forwarded the work.[2] The likeness of the east trio of lancets to those at Graignamanagh suggests an earlier date for them than Bishop Hugh's episcopate, but there can be little doubt that the nave of the church was completed by *c.* 1275, while St. Leger (1260-86) held the see. The arcades are shown in Plate XVIIIb.

Less affected by modern restoration than the Dublin cathedrals St. Canices is not so rich in detail as the nave of Christ Church nor so austere as the greater part of St. Patrick's. Influenced by both in some degree it strikes a happy compromise in its serene beauty and coherence of design. In length—224 feet overall—it is second among the Irish medieval cathedrals. The church (50) is cruciform with a central tower. It has aisles to the nave of five bays and the peculiar, almost Cistercian feature, of transept chapels *en echelon*. The longer chapels adjoin the choir and are open to it through arcades of two arches. In effect they are choir aisles and extensions of those of the nave though a little wider than the latter. Open to the transept only is the smaller north chapel. It is balanced on the south side of the choir aisle by a large, many-windowed Lady Chapel of later thirteenth-century date.

The construction is, as usual, of limestone rubble with dressings of sandstone and limestone. In the choir the former is used exclusively and, externally, the sandstone dressings extend to the western face of the tower. Westwards from this point, however, limestone preponderates both within and without. There are broad buttresses of small projection clasping all the main external angles except at the west end of the nave where they project strongly, become octagonal in plan near the top, and are capped by tall pyramids (Pl. XVIIIa).

The choir (Pl. XVIIIb) is lighted by a graduated trio of pointed windows in the east wall, similar triplets—but with round heads—

in the north and south walls, and a row of five, small pointed lights on each side above the chapel roofs. Moulded and dog-tooth decorated rear-arches of foliated form (the centre arch is stilted) span the inner embrasures of the east windows which have detached jamb and pier shafts of marble, banded and bearing stiff-leaf foliage capitals. High in the gable is a circular octofoiled light. The north and south windows have trefoiled rear-arches and interior trim similar to the east windows. There is some doubt as to the authenticity of the clearstorey windows over the chapel roofs; all are pointed within and without but are restorations of 1866 and while it is possible that some traces of them survived the fall of the central tower in 1332 it is recorded that there were two square-topped windows on each side before the restoration. In the north, south and west walls of the transept are lancets in pairs, shafted internally, and similar undecorated shorter lancets light the small north chapel. In the larger north chapel the east window is a group of three pointed lights in the one embrasure which has a rear arcade, and the north windows are three in number, each of a pair of lights with a quatrefoil over. These embrasures have nook-shafts in pairs, foliage and nail-head capitals and moulded rear-arches. The grouping of lights in all these windows can hardly be earlier than the mid-century. The Lady Chapel—now the Chapter Room—was in very bad condition in 1866 and it was entirely rebuilt in the restoration, using the original materials. " More glass than wall " it was perhaps the best-lighted erection in medieval Ireland, but it had a very close competitor in the Lady Chapel of another church in Kilkenny—that of St. John's Priory (*post* p. 109). Its entire south wall is filled by lancets, separated by mullions, graded and grouped in threes internally and externally. The central light in each trio is higher and wider than the others. Similar windows but grouped in pairs with a quatrefoil over fill the east wall. The central pair is higher than the others. This work is in limestone throughout, a circumstance which, combined with the grouping, places it in the later part of the century; coeval with, or perhaps a little later than the nave.

The transept windows have been mentioned already. It remains to note two other features: the very fine tomb recess in the north wall, all in limestone (Pl. XXa) with its foiled, moulded arch and hood-moulding, carved heads as stops to the latter, and foliage-carved capitals and marble detached shafts flanked by dog-tooth ornament. Quite possibly this was the burial place of Bishop Hugh de Mapilton. The other feature is the north door. It is round-arched and set in a recess with a pointed arch. This has engaged jamb-shafts, foliage-caps and a moulded archivolt, but the doorway has engaged and filleted shafts with numerous delicate bands. This treatment is carried round the arch beneath a quatrefoil.

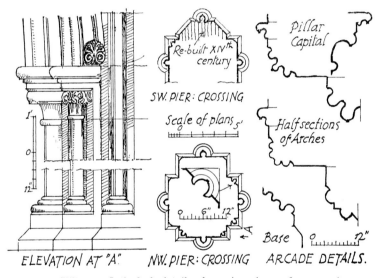

51. Kilkenny Cathedral: details of crossing piers and nave arches

Of the four piers of the crossing only that at the north-west preserves its original plan: of broad cross form with engaged shafts central in each face (51). The south-west pier is original on its west side but altered on the east. It was partly rebuilt (c. 1354) after the belfry tower fell in 1332. At the same time the eastern piers were entirely reconstructed on a quite different plan—with all their responds widely splayed, the engaged shafts being repeated. Several of the main arches the piers support are made up of moulded voussoirs alternately of sandstone and limestone: evidence of the re-use of original stones. The thirteenth-century tower was higher than as rebuilt and may not have had a vault over the crossing where is now Bishop Hackett's—fifteenth-century—star vault.

The five-bayed nave is a little over 100 feet in length. Pillars of quatrefoil plan, 20 feet apart, with moulded capitals (51), carry arches of two orders and in the clearstorey are large quatrefoil windows with segmental-pointed rear-arches. Three fine graduated lancets in the west wall have unornamented embrasures but at the base of the central one is a very curious feature: a small inner arcade of two trefoiled arches beneath a larger arch and quatrefoil. Beneath the three foiled round lights in a panel, at the back of this arcade, is the elaborate west doorway (Pl. XIX). It has twin openings with pointed, cinque-foiled heads in a main recess of two arches (52) carried by nook shafts in pairs, with moulded and foliage-carved caps. There is a central shaft between the openings around which run delicate mouldings. In the tympanum are shallow niches: a large quatrefoil in the centre; flanked by four roundels and two foiled circles. The larger niche perhaps had a carving of the Virgin and Child, since in the others there are weathered carvings of adoring angels. There is a steeply-gabled south porch central in the aisle. Its outer arch—of two orders, moulded—springs from capitals with small tonsured and mitred heads amid rich foliage. There were marble nook-shafts below. These were repeated, singly, in the jambs of the simpler inner doorway which, again, is repeated in the north aisle opposite. The windows of the aisles are coupled lancets beneath a central quatrefoil and a hood-mould: a form of plate tracery. Trefoil form rear-arches span the inner embrasures except those at the west end which are pointed. Multi-stepped battlements surmount the walls of nave, choir and transept as well as the very low tower.[3]

4-foil Panel

Main Arch

0   6"   12"

KILKENNY CATHL.
W. DOORWAY MDGS.

52
Kilkenny Cathedral:
mouldings of west
doorway

Plate XVIII

XVIIIa.　Exterior from South-west

XVIIIb.　Interior, looking North-east and South-east

ST. CANICE'S CATHEDRAL, KILKENNY

PLATE XIX

XIX. ST. CANICE'S CATHEDRAL, KILKENNY

West Doorway

Both the city and county of Kilkenny are rich in works of the period. In the city, on the other side of the river to the cathedral, are the remains of the church of the Augustinian priory of St. John the Evangelist. The earlier part, the east end, retains a remarkable window filling the whole wall. It is a double composition of triplets with foliated heads and varied in width and height (Pl. XVb). Banded jamb and central shafts carry the pair of moulded rear-arches (53) complete with hood-mouldings. A small foiled circle fills the gable and two twin-light windows with bar tracery flank the altar on the south. The dating of this part of the church, the choir, is in doubt. It is unlikely that it is so early as 1220, the accepted foundation date; even in England the grouping of lancets in one composition and divided only by mullions does not occur so early. Round about the mid-century would be an acceptable date for this work. The two south windows with their simple bar or switch-line-tracery present a more serious problem. Such windows were common, as will be seen later (p. 125), at the end of the century; their appearance at Kilkenny *c.* 1250 is remarkable. But the interior trim of these windows: moulded rear-arches of much the same section as those of the east window, the vortex-like foliage

53
Kilkenny, St. John's
Priory Church:
east window details

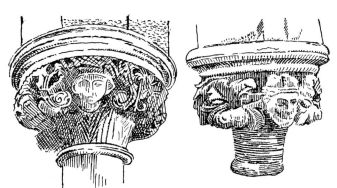

CASHEL CATHL: CAP KILKENNY: CAP IN
TO ARCH: S. PORCH S. WINDOW, ST. JOHN'S.

54. Capitals with faces in foliage

capitals (54) which accord with the date of the window seem conclusive. It is just conceivable, however, that the tracery was inserted in place of original lancets but structural evidence is lacking.

To the south lies the Lady Chapel (now the Protestant Church) known in its day as " the Lantern of Ireland " from the multitude of its windows. Its whole south wall, reconstructed in 1817, is filled with close-set, trefoil-pointed lights in threes, five groups in all, the centre light in each higher than its fellows. Two of the groups are now built up. In the east wall is a three-light Geometrical tracery (switch-line) window of the form common from c. 1300. It is presumably an insertion of that period. As to the date of the Lady Chapel the stylistic indications place it in the later decades of the century. It may well have been inspired by the many-windowed Lady Chapel at St. Canice's and be datable to c. 1280.

It is curious that as late as the middle of the century a vogue for round-headed windows should survive here and there. St. Canice's, for instance, has six. The church of the Franciscans at BUTTEVANT, Cork, has a close-set row of eight—not as lofty as the triplets at Kilkenny—south of the choir. They contrast with the three lancets in the east wall, three south of the transept and two in the west gable. All these pointed windows have been built up or covered, or have had fifteenth-century lights inserted in them. The friary was founded by a de Barry about 1250 on the edge of his town and on a site sloping rather steeply to the bank of the Awbeg river. It is a typical friars' church, a long rectangle with a south wing or transept to the nave. This wing is not much later in date than the nave. It seems to have been contemplated from the first and is an early appearance of a feature which was to become invariable in friars' churches though it cannot differ much in date from the south wing of St. Dominick's church at Cashel (*ante* p. 93). The central tower, which fell in 1819, may also have been intended from the first. An old engraving shows it as having banded angle-shafts, unique in Irish towers and perhaps an indication of thirteenth-century date. Another almost unique feature is the crypt, an affair of two storeys, beneath the east end. It can have no liturgical significance, rather was it the inevitable consequence of the rapid eastward fall of the ground. Central in the upper crypt is a stout pillar of curious plan: four half-round shafts separated by hollows in which stood free shafts. The capital has stiff-leaf foliage carving. Seen from the south the aspect of the church is semi-military. This is due to the heavy walling (fifteenth-century) which covers the end of the south transept. Between its two parts is a recess, arched at the top, in which can be seen the original central lancet, partly closed and altered. A high talus batter adds to the castle-like effect which suggests that the friary was incorporated in the southern defences of the town.

In distant Kerry, but in parts by then subject to Anglo-Norman power, two interesting buildings were erected in the prevailing style. The first is the cathedral of St. Brendan at ARDFERT which took the place of the earlier church now represented by the Romanesque west doorway and blank arcades described already (Vol. I, pp. 124-5). In plan the church is very simple: a long rectangle with a short south aisle (the south wing is much later), very like a friars' church. Probably it owes its origin to Bishop Christian (1252-6), a Dominican, who may well have caused the church to be built on the lines he had been familiar with as a friar. Three fine graduated lancets—the centre light about 27 feet in height—rise high into the gable and dominate the east end (55). Their internal jamb and pier shafts, the latter double, are four times banded and have small capitals, with delicate, rather early-looking foliage, from which the moulded rear-arches spring. There are hood-mouldings to these and to the arched niches (very similar in detail to the window trim) which flank the composition. Externally the lights have broad chamfers all round and are set in recesses bordered with a small, double-rolled moulding—the latest appearance of the western " frame " ? Massive square buttresses—over 5 feet in width and projecting 2 feet—clasp the

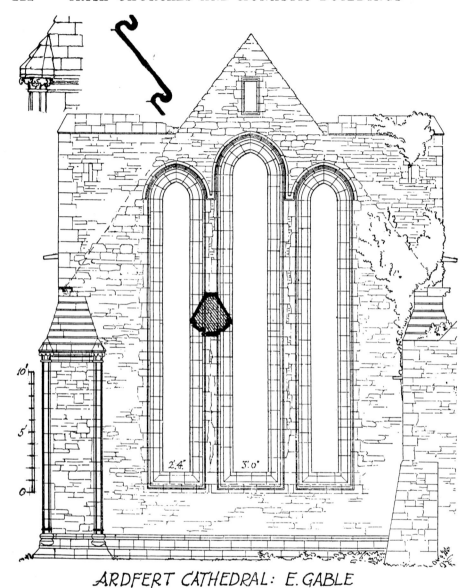

ARDFERT CATHEDRAL: E. GABLE

55. Ardfert Cathedral: elevation of east gable (after Hill)

quoins and die back into the walls in a high pyramid of moulded weather-courses. Engaged with the angles of the buttresses are

PLATE XX

XXb. ARDFERT CATHEDRAL

Tomb Recess in North Transept

XXa. ST. CANICE'S CATHEDRAL, KILKENNY

Interior of Choir, looking South-east

Plate XXI

XXIb. GOWRAN CHURCH

Interior of Nave, Looking West

XXIa. ARDFERT FRIARY CHURCH

Interior of Choir, Looking South-east

thrice-filleted shafts rising from bases, wrought in the double base-course, to foliage-carved capitals coincident with a cornice.

Striking as is the eastern internal composition still more so is the row of nine lancets occupying the whole south wall. Their moulded, trefoiled rear-arches and banded pier-shafts make a continuous arcade. The shafts are set on a moulded string at the bottom of the sill-splays. This string steps up in the centre of the fourth embrasure over the remnants of the sediliæ and piscina recesses. A half-arch of the former, which was triple, has bold dog-tooth ornament which is repeated in the arches of the nearby niches (Pl. XXb).

The brilliantly-lighted choir must have been in strong contrast with a rather dim nave lit only by low windows in the south aisle, three small windows near the centre of the church, another over the west door (all of them have gone) and the still existing twin lights high in the north wall. Between nave and choir pairs of corbels mark the site of a timber rood loft.

In few of the churches so far discussed do there remain clear indications of the form of construction of the timber roofs. At Ardfert there is one: the horizontal offset just above the lancets within the east gable. It marks the position of the cross-tie or collar of a very simple type of roof, probably of heavy couples set close together and without principals at intervals.

Stepped battlements of obviously defensive character rise to a considerable height—14 feet—above the thirteenth-century eaves-line and all of the many gargoyles of the later stone guttering remain. These wall-tops are either of the fourteenth century or, more probably, of the 1400's, as are the sacristy building to the north-east and the south wing with its east chapel. The south aisle has gone but its arcade of three pointed, chamfered arches, rising from square piers, also chamfered at the angles beneath corbel-like imposts, remains.

Remarkably similar in size and details to the cathedral is the church of the Franciscan friary of ARDFERT (Pl. XXIa) not far distant. Reliable documentary evidence for the date of its erection is lacking but the architectural evidence suggests that the cathedral served as a model for the friary church. The 1260's may well be the appropriate period; the founder is said to have been buried there in 1280.[5]

It is a friars' church; a long rectangle without a stone-built division between nave and choir. In the south wall of the latter, as in the cathedral—are nine lancets in a row with trefoiled rear-arches (slightly pointed, however) with chamfers dying into the plain splays. The east windows are five in number, all lancets subtly graduated, divided by narrow piers. These are simply chamfered but there are banded shafts to the two side-splays. The arcade of three pointed arches on round piers to the vanished south aisle remains. Their rather coarsely moulded bases and capitals suggest a date not earlier—and quite possibly later—than the fourteenth century for the aisle. Certainly of the fifteenth century is the transept, with its round arched arcade to a west aisle and windows, not within the scope of this chapter. Of the same period is the tower at the west end, a position unique in Irish friaries. It and the claustral buildings will also be dealt with later.

At NENAGH (Tipperary) in the ruined church of the Franciscan friary (the claustral buildings which lay to the south have gone) there is the longest row of conjoined lancets, eleven in number, in the north wall of the choir, all very plainly treated. In the east wall there are, as usual, three graduated lancets of large size. Nenagh friary, founded by the O Kennedys in the mid-century, was the head of a *custodium* of the Order in 1262 and the church is probably of about that date.

The church of the Dominican friary at ROSCOMMON is securely dated. This friary was founded in 1253,[6] the church being consecrated in 1257.[7] In it the founder, Felim O Conor, Lord of Roscommon and quondam king of Connacht, was buried in 1265.[8]

It had lancets to east and west (replaced in the fifteenth century by large tracery windows, since destroyed). There was a row of lancets in the north wall but these, too, have been largely destroyed. There are several remaining in the south wall of the nave overlooking the cloister, of which scarcely a trace remains. There was an aisle to the nave and parts of the fifteenth-century north wing still stand. The most interesting relic is the effigy of Felim which lies in a niche north of the high altar site above the well-known frontal stone with gallowglass figures, part of a later tomb.

At SLIGO the remains of the church and other buildings of another Dominican friary are more extensive. In 1252, Maurice Fitzgerald, who had been justiciary of Ireland, founded the friary. Belonging to this period are the north and south walls of the choir, the north wall of the nave and some parts of the sacristy and chapter house. A row of eight lancets, with sandstone trimmings fills the south wall of the choir, and there are three pairs of lights in the nave wall, but all in limestone, as well as a triplet (now blocked up) in the chapter house. The numerous alterations of later centuries belong to another chapter but may be summarized here: the east window in place of the original lancets; the central tower and the remains of a vaulted rood screen; the added south aisle and transept.

At LORRHA, Tipperary, a church for the Dominicans was built in 1269. Like that at Sligo it is a plain, rather severe structure but there is a change in the fenestration of the choir: the lancets are in pairs, not single but still regularly spaced, the inner embrasures in enfilade, as usual. There was a stone screen or pulpitum—but apparently no tower—midway in the length of the church.

In 1272 Archbishop David MacCarvill (who ruled at Cashel from 1253 to 1289) because of a vision which warned him that the Benedictines (presumably the Order still persisted at the Rock) were plotting to kill him, ejected them and built a new monastery for Cistercians at HORE (4), in the plain below the Rock. It was the last Cistercian foundation and was colonized by monks from Mellifont. The building dates from soon after 1272 and follows the usual plan except in having the cloister and its ranges, now almost destroyed, to the north of the church. The presbytery is short and there were two square chapels in each arm of the transept. Of these chapels only the north pair remains, each covered by a pointed barrel-vault. At the quoins of the presbytery and south transept are pairs of salient buttresses in weathered stages. All the walling and the trim of the plain and not numerous lancets—a trio to the east, a pair in the transept gable, a tall single light in the west wall and other single lights elsewhere—are in limestone. That the work is stylistically the same as the nave of the cathedral is obvious and the presence of the same masons' marks in both buildings makes it clear that there can be no great difference in their dates. The central tower is an insertion of the fifteenth century, as are the small windows, in several storeys, which fill the tall embrasure of the nave's west window.

In strong contrast to this austere Cistercian structure is the collegiate church of St. Mary the Virgin at GOWRAN (Kilkenny), a building of c. 1275, rich in the quality of its details which owe something to the Christ Church style. A late tower divides the aisled and roofless nave from the modern church which stands on the site of the original chancel. In the west wall of the nave is a triplet of grace and beauty (Pl. XXIb) with trefoil-pointed heads to the lights and rear-arches. The latter are moulded and there are hood-mouldings within and without. The internal shafting is banded and its capitals foliage-carved. Carved heads form the stops and the composition is completed by a round, sex-foiled light high in the gable. At each end of the aisles are twin lights, also trefoil-pointed, with a quatrefoil over, similar, except for the heads, to the aisle windows at Kilkenny cathedral. Those to the east have inner arcades (Pl. XXIIIa): a central pillar bearing moulded, trefoiled arches and a central quatrefoil. Multi-foiled arches span (Pl. XXVIIIc) tomb recesses in the south aisle wall. Only the north aisle arcade still stands. It has pillars of quatrefoil plan (as at Kilkenny) and plain chamfered arches springing from moulded capitals. In the clearstorey, below stepped battlements, are quatrefoil windows with segmental-pointed rear-arches.

At THOMASTOWN (Kilkenny) there remain the north wall of the nave and the choir arch of the parish church, a structure of about the same date as that at Gowran but more severe in its detail. One round and three quatrefoil-planned pillars carry the plain chamfered arches—five in number—of the arcade over the piers of which (in Cistercian fashion) are the clearstorey windows. These are pairs of lancets. Some of the pier capitals are moulded; others have compact foliage. There was an altar at the end of the north aisle with a two-light window over it and a piscina in the adjoining respond of the arcade, and, in the south pier of the chancel arch—a plain pointed affair—is a doorway leading to the winding stairs which gave access to the roof-walk. This retains a stepped parapet wall of the usual Irish type. Only foundations mark the rest of the church: the chancel and sacristy, a detached chapel south of the former and the tower at the west end of the south aisle. But some of the west wall still stands, pierced by a doorway of uncertain date.

Large parish churches of the thirteenth century, like those of Gowran and Thomastown, were of rare occurrence in Ireland and were confined to the towns controlled by the Anglo-Normans. Few survive: in Dublin only a part of St. Audoen's remains; that of St. Mary in Kilkenny has been drastically altered though retaining its cruciform plan; so also does the large church at Youghal of the same dedication, but it has been altered and extended at later periods; St. Nicholas at Dundalk has also been very much altered and extended, and the large parish church of St. Peter, Drogheda, was demolished in the eighteenth century.

But the conquerors were also largely responsible for the founding of monasteries in addition to those already described, far away from towns. One such was Dominican RATHFRAN (Mayo) near the shore of Killala Bay. Founded by either a de Burgh or a MacJordan in 1274, it was a large establishment with two courtyards north of the church, one the cloister garth, the other, further north, apparently domestic in use. Both, with their surrounding ranges, are now represented by foundations only. The not large church is a plain rectangle with a short, narrow south aisle of later date. In the east wall are the remains of a triplet of trefoil-pointed lights in a wide embrasure with banded, engaged shafts to the jambs, and in the south wall are five pairs of lancets—as at Lorrha—four of them close-set in a row, evenly spaced. Alongside a round-headed sedilia there is a piscina niche with a foliated arch and there are similarly arched tomb recesses.

AT CLOYNE (Cork) the cathedral is also probably of the 1270's. It is a cruciform church which had narrow aisles to its five-bayed nave. The arcade of plain pointed arches is very simple; the piers are rectangular and merely chamfered at the angles. Most noticeable are the windows of the south transept: five graduated, trefoil-pointed lancets (now built up), grouped in the gable, and a triplet, flanked by similar pairs, in the east wall (Pl. XXII). The north transept is less brightly lighted; it has but one foliated triplet to the east and three tall lancets to the north. The close grouping of lights divided only by mullions first makes its appearance about the middle of the century (cf. St. John's, Kilkenny, *ante* p. 109); but in its closing decades mullion-divided windows become normal. In most of the churches built before *c.* 1270 the characteristic eastern window group was of lancets—three or five in number—separated by piers of about the same width as the lights, externally, but triangular in plan; only on the inner elevation do the five or three become a unit. In the closing years of the century internal and external unity became normal in the design of these important windows: by a close grouping of the lights, the massive dividing piers giving place to relatively slender mullions and the three or five inner arches to one spanning the wide inner embrasure.

Two examples illustrate this important development: the church of the Franciscan friary at ENNIS (Clare) and that of the

Dominicans at Kilmallock (Limerick). Ennis friary was first founded about 1240 or 1247: but it is not certain or probable that the church was then completed. If so it must have suffered great damage in the following turbulent decades when the kings of Thomond were engaged in petty wars. In 1285, however, King Turloch (Toirdhealbhach) set about expelling the Anglo-Normans from Thomond, a task which took twenty years to accomplish. He died in 1306 and was buried in the friary church not far from the great east window (56) which, it is recorded, he had built and filled with painted blue glass.[10] This window seems to be an intermediate

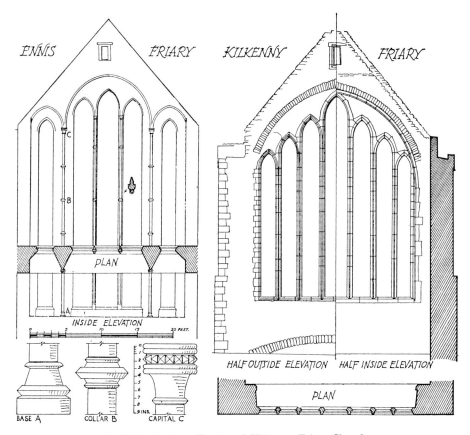

56.　East windows: Ennis and Kilkenny Friary Churches

stage in the development. It has five lights but only the central three are mullioned and grouped together; the side lights are single but the piers between them and the centre group are much more slender than those in any earlier buildings with the one exception of Ardfert friary of *c.* 1260-70. The central lancet is but 2 ft. 8 ins. wide and rises to a height of 30 feet; the dividing mullions have a slender pipe-like roll or shaft on the inner nib as also have the piers. All these shafts are banded at intervals and those of the mullions finish in heads or ornaments, while from the moulded and dog-tooth ornamented capitals of the main shafts spring the moulded rear-arches of all three embrasures. In the south wall of the choir the windows—five in number, four of them coupled lancets, the fifth a triplet—are more widely spaced than in the friary churches so far described.

In the second example, the nearly coeval (between 1291 and *c.* 1300) church of the Dominicans at KILMALLOCK, however, the *enfilade* of windows appears again. There are six in the row, all originally of two lights, mullioned and with switch-line tracery. The great window filling the east wall (Pl. XXIV) focusses interest. Its five lancets, separated only by mullions and graduated in height and width, make an impressive group beneath the single rear-arch spanning the 18-feet-wide inner embrasure. The mullions, as at Ennis, have banded shafts on the inner edges, finishing in moulded capitals, as do the jamb-shafts, also banded, to the embrasure. There is a hood-moulding, with carved heads as stops, to the moulded rear-arch. The south transept with its west aisle, as well as the adjoining aisle to the nave, are fourteenth-century works and belong to the following chapter.

The friary is outside the once walled town of Kilmallock: capital of the Earls of Desmond. Within it are the remains of a large parish church dedicated to SS. Peter and Paul and in the gable of its choir is a five-light window very similar to and perhaps inspired by that at the friary and probably of about the same date. The nave has wide aisles—obviously additions but of doubtful date—and, in the west wall are the remains of a doorway of the thirteenth century. There is a short south transept and a fifteenth-century porch and doorway. The most curious feature of the structure is the altered and truncated round tower at the north-west angle incorporated in the later work and used as a belfry.

Near the head of Bannow Bay, Wexford, are the remains of the abbey church of TINTERN MINOR. The Cistercian house here was founded by William the Earl Marshal about the year 1200, in the fulfilment of a vow he made during a very stormy crossing from England and hence called, in the Cistercian annals, *Votum* or *de Voto*. The first monks came from Tintern, in Monmouthshire.

Within the extant building the post-Dissolution grantee built a dwelling, part of which (in the nave) is still lived in by a descendant. These remains—the presbytery, crossing, tower, south transept and nave (now without its aisles)—are much later than the foundation date. The wide east window of the presbytery which now lacks its Geometrical tracery, and the form of the salient buttresses with gablets to each offset closely resemble the same features in the great Monmouthshire church, the parent house, built between 1269 and *c.* 1288. The Irish building is, therefore, datable to the late thirteenth century. Tudor, mullioned lights in the built-up side windows show that lay owners inserted several storeys of apartments within the presbytery. The massive central tower—possibly original and if so a departure from early Cistercian usages—has Irish crenellation. In the pseudo-Gothic reconstruction of the south transept the chapels were not altered.

1. *Nomina Eporum Ossorien*, MS. T.C.D., E3. 13. *fol.* 88.

2. Ware-Harris; I, p. 403-6.

3. Graves and Prim: *History and Antiquities of the Cathedral Church of St. Canice, Kilkenny* (1857), p. 80.

4. *ibid.* See also Clapham: *Arch. Jour.*, cvi, pp. 33-6; and Leask: *J.R.S.A.I.* 79 (1949) pp. 1-9.

5. Lodge: *Peerage*, II, p. 102. 6. Ware-Harris, II, p. 277.

7. *Annals of Loch Cé*, I, p. 425. 8. *Ann. Four Masters*, III, p. 397.

9. *ibid.*

10. *Wars of Turlogh* (Cathreim Thoirdhealbhaigh) and Annals of Innisfallen.

Chapter VII

IRISH GOTHIC IN THE FOURTEENTH CENTURY

In the later decades of the thirteenth century there was some slackening in building activity; through the years from 1300 to 1350 it is more marked—fewer new structures were raised or older ones added to than in the middle decades of the preceding hundred years. The reasons are to be found in the Irish history of the period. It is true that the greater lords—the fitzGeralds and the Butlers, for instance, whom we may now call the Anglo-Irish—were increasing in power but that of the royal government, vacillating, inconsistent and often misguided, was on the wane. By themselves these circumstances might have been no great deterrent to ecclesiastical building but there was much strife as well. This was intensified in 1315 by the invasion of Edward Bruce bent on making or taking a kingdom for himself. In the three and a half years of his campaigning before he met defeat and death at Faughart in 1318 " famine and general ruin "[1] came to a large area extending from Ulster to the midlands. Nor was this the only war in progress; some of the lords de Bermingham and de Burgh marched on a Connacht resurgent in the confusion and defeated a large Irish force in an exceedingly bloody battle at Athenry in 1316. Two years later, on the native side, the resurgent O Briens broke the forty-year-old Anglo-Norman grip on the kingdom of Thomond.

These all too brief and generalized sentences must serve to illustrate the state of the greater part of Ireland in the second and third decades of the century; greater catastrophe was still to come. In 1348 the pestilence, the Black Death, reached Britain and, before long, Ireland also. It was raging in the towns—the main centres of building activity—in 1349 and brought building to a standstill, on any considerable scale, for more than half a century.

It is not surprising that, in the circumstances outlined, the number of buildings erected or even added to in the period should be small; scarcely a dozen can be ascribed, with full confidence, to the fourteenth century and few of these to the years following Bruce's invasion or the later part of the century.

Architectural fashion changes are well exemplified in window design and it was in the early 1300's that window tracery made its appearance in Ireland, if we exclude the two-light, switch-line windows at Kilkenny and Kilmallock from the definition of the term. Tracery, which may be defined, shortly, as openwork of stone filling the upper part of a window in continuation of the mullions, began to develop in English architecture just before the middle of the thirteenth century as windows increased in width. It progressed from geometrical designs (mainly arch forms enclosing multi-cusped circles) through a phase in which the circular forms are less dominant and the geometrical figures employed (trefoils, quatrefoils, lozenges, etc.) form the main lines of the design. The pointed-trefoil (59) appears about 1290-1300. These two phases are usually termed " Early and Late Geometrical " and with that which succeeds them—the " Curvilinear "—make up the style commonly designated " Decorated." In the Curvilinear phase, as the title suggests, the bars of the stonework follow flowing curves and the ogee form (65, 77) appears. The Decorated period was that in which, in England, tracery design was developing rapidly in bewildering variety. In Ireland the change was less rapid and was expressed in fewer forms. The lancet, single or grouped, persisted; indeed, it never quite passed out of use in Irish work. The largest window—the east window of the Franciscan church at Kilkenny (56)—which is made up of seven large lancets, grouped, was erected in 1321 when the choir was extended, and single and paired lancets are to be found in many fifteenth-century churches. What is known as plate-tracery, a type which preceded Decorated, does not occur in pure form in Irish work; the nearest approaches to it are the aisle windows in Kilkenny cathedral and Gowran church already mentioned. These windows are pairs of lancets, foliated at Gowran, with a quatrefoil above and an enclosing hood-mould.

There is another type of window which may be regarded as the beginning of tracery in a real sense. It has been mentioned already (pp. 109) appearing in the south walls of St. John's church, Kilkenny, and Kilmallock friary: a pair of lancets formed by the divergence to right and left of the dividing mullion. It is not found in Britain before c. 1260 and the date of its Irish appearance is probably somewhat later. The system as applied to three or more lights is first found in English Gothic around the year 1300.

In principle this design is very simple: each mullion branches into curves of exactly the same radius as the enclosing arch against which each curved bar terminates. The result is quite logical if uninspired, and the cost of construction low in comparison with that of more elaborate designs. Such tracery has been variously named: " intersecting-bar " or " switch-line." The latter term, if inelegant, is expressive to modern ears and will be used in the pages which follow. What appears to be its earliest Irish appearance in three-light windows is in the east windows (Pl. XXIIIb) of the three chapels of the large transept added to CASTLEDERMOT friary church in the early years of the century; perhaps—absolute dating is not possible—in 1302 when the originally poor friary was well endowed. The transept is the most elaborate of those added to friars' churches. In addition to the chapels it had a west aisle and the treatment of the arcade to them is inspired by the architecture of St. Patrick's, Dublin; the little niches over the piers are almost copies of those in the triforium stage of the Dublin cathedral. It is unfortunate that the tracery of the large north window was deliberately demolished in the early 1800's, but some fragments remain. There is a rather crude engraving in Grose's *Antiquities of Ireland*. There were four plain, paired lights surmounted by a spherical-triangle centre-piece, sex-foiled. In the spandrel below this was a trefoil but the side-spandrels or eyes were unpierced. It was a fine example of the Geometrical phase, simplified in detail for execution in granite. About the same time the choir was lengthened eastwards but of the large east window then built only the jambs remain. It possibly resembled the north window.

Switch-line tracery was to become the normal form for windows of three or more lights in width in the fifteenth century but in its fourteenth-century manifestations the mullions and bars are noticeably stouter than they are in the later work. Just such heavy bars are to be seen in two south windows of the choir of the cathedral at OLD LEIGHLIN (Carlow) and in the eastern arm of the church of the Augustinian friary, the " Black Abbey " (now the Protestant church) at ADARE (Limerick) (Pl. XXIVb).

This church is " one of the few outstanding examples of definitely fourteenth-century date in Ireland."[2] Its foundation date is c. 1316 but that of its completion is less certain. However, since the district and the patrons were wealthy, and the grants fully adequate, no great delay in building the church (the claustral buildings are later) need be postulated. Possibly 1320-25 is not far wide of the mark. The five-light east window and the narrower south windows of the choir are all of switch-line form, and the mullions and bars are broad and rebated to take glazing frames (as in earlier work) and have a round member on the external nibs. In plan the church is of the friars' type but there appears to have been a narrow, south aisle to the nave from the first. It was replaced by a wider aisle in the following century in which, also, the claustral ranges and the belfry tower were built.

The simple tracery at Adare was to be elaborated in other churches, for instance that of the Dominicans at ATHENRY (Galway) (57, 58). In 1324 the Athenry friary church was extended to the east by about 20 feet. At that time, or perhaps a little later, an aisle and transept were added north of the nave. In the choir extension, on the right and left of the altar, is a window

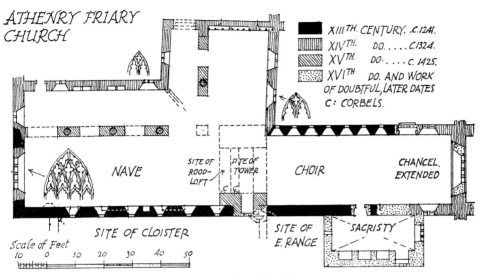

57. Athenry Friary Church: plan

two lights wide. The south window (58c) has switch-line tracery enclosing foliated lights and a small trefoil; its centrepiece is a multifoiled circle. In the other window (58b) the lights are also foliated but the centrepiece is a sex-foiled spherical triangle. The aisle-windows are also of two lights with a pointed quatrefoil over the double-cusped foliated lights (58a). The large east window, now destroyed except for its outer and rear-arches, was ambitious in design. One restoration has been attempted from the surviving connections of the tracery with the outer arch.[3] Closer study and measurement indicate that the window was of five lights in width, not six. The tracery was of switch-line design in part, with modifications as well as cusping to the apertures. Tentative restoration is profitless. One feature certainly occurs: the pointed trefoil. This appeared in English windows towards the end of the thirteenth century and persisted for some decades. It is a sure mark of fourteenth-century work in Ireland. Of the nearly coeval large but more simply designed window of the north transept loose fragments remain. The bars are broad and roll-moulded externally. These,

fig 3 Window tracery

58. Athenry Friary Church: windows in extended chancel, etc.
(*a*) in north aisle; (*b* and *c*) in north and south walls

together with the surviving jambs, show that the tracery was of spherical triangles, two small and one large, all cusped and sexfoiled.

These features of Athenry are outdone in variety of design and elaboration by the windows of the other Dominican church, that at KILKENNY, known as the " Black Abbey." The remarkably long south transept is not dated by any documentary evidence but the elaborated tracery in its large south window (Pl. XXVa) suggests that it is later in date than the work of 1324 at Athenry. The window is the largest of its type, filling almost the whole of the gable wall. It is five lights in width. These have pointed heads with a suggestion of the ogee at the points. The mullions branch in switch-lines and in the resulting apertures cusps make the upper lozenge-shaped openings into pointed quatrefoils, contrasting with the quatrefoiled circles below. In the openings above the main lights cusping produces a curious figure (59)—pointed above,

PLATE XXII

XXIIa.   East Side of South Transept

PLATE XXIII

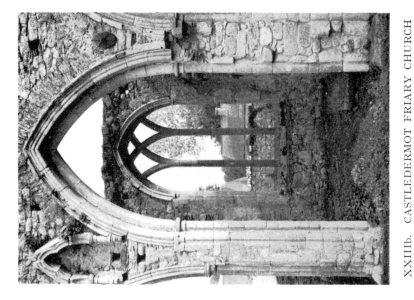

XXIIIb. CASTLEDERMOT FRIARY CHURCH

Arcade of Transept Chapels

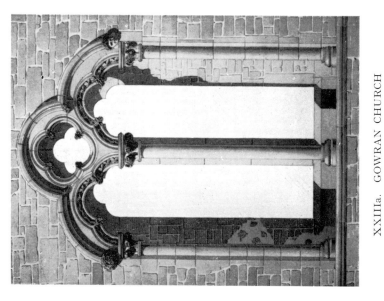

XXIIIa. GOWRAN CHURCH

East Window of South Aisle

circular below. There are in the side-wall of the transept four (originally five) three-light windows of varied design. One, of switch-line type, has pointed trefoils and quatrefoils; another, with foliated lights, has a circular centrepiece enclosing three spherical triangles, trefoiled. Another window of later type adjoins these fourteenth-century designs. In it the ogee form of heads to the lights is to be seen. This combination of reversed curves appears in Britain at *c.* 1310 in the chapel of Merton College, Oxford. It is the distinguishing mark of the curvilinear phase of the Decorated style and remained in use, even in the latest phase— the Perpendicular—of English Gothic. It was equally long-lived in Ireland.

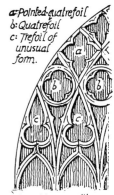

KILKENNY: DOM.ᶜᴺ CH. S. WINDOW TRACERY

59. Kilekenny "Black Abbey": tracery of south window

The Kilkenny transept with its south window was probably the last major work of the half-century before the plague came, but some lesser works of the period, a few of them earlier in date, remain to be noticed. Among them are two windows at FETHARD in Tipperary. Both are of three lights with foliated heads. In the switch-line tracery above the foliated heads of one are pointed trefoils, and two quatrefoiled circles below a pointed quatrefoil in the apex (60); in the other, similar lights are surmounted by multi-foiled circles. The priory was founded for Augustinians in 1306 but these advanced windows are, perhaps, somewhat later than that date. The Cistercians at Jerpoint inserted a three-light window in the east gable in place of the original Romanesque three. It has multifoiled heads to its lights, beneath a circle originally filled with whirling, comma-shaped apertures (61). The hood has the ball-flower ornament. To accommodate this centre-piece the heads of the side-lights diverge to right and left. Unique in Ireland though it be this design is hardly satisfactory. At the mother-house of the same Order, Mellifont, the chapter house received an eastern extension, vaulted in two bays with moulded cross-, wall- and diagonal ribs rising from triple wall-shafts (62). The side windows (Pl. XXVIb) have curvilinear tracery of a form which became common in the next century. All the members are

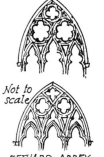

Not to scale

FETHARD ABBEY NAVE WINDOWS
60

"Ballflower" ornamᵗ

CONJᵗ. RESTⁿ. JERPOINT: E. WINDOW
61

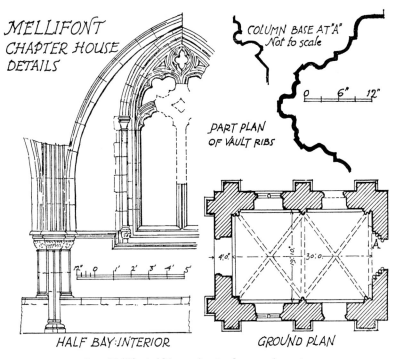

62.   Mellifont Abbey: chapter house, plan, etc.

KILMALLOCK: TRANST.
63

CLAREGALWAY: NAVE
64

moulded and the openings multi-cusped. A curious survival from an earlier style is the dog-tooth or large nail-head motive worked on the inner moulded jamb-stones. Of the same period are some alterations to the south transept where new piers of clustered plan were built between the chapels. Several piers on the south side of the nave were of the same plan.

An aisle was added to the nave of CLAREGALWAY friary. Its arcade stands (63). The pillars are cylindrical, with moulded capitals of simple section, and the arches, in two orders, are chamfered. At the friary church of the Dominicans in KILMALLOCK also, a transept with a west aisle was added. The single pillar in the aisle arcade (64) is round, as at Claregalway, but its capital is bolder and exhibits one of the two Irish occurrences of the ball-flower ornament so popular in English Gothic in the early fourteenth century. One small window with two foliated lights is coeval with the arcade, but the great, five-light south window of the transept, with its curvilinear, net-like tracery is too similar to many windows of the fifteenth century not to be an insertion of that period. To accommodate it almost all of the wall must have been reconstructed.

The rather lengthy consideration given already to switch-line tracery and its development must not be taken as indicating that it is the only form found. One, the spherical triangle, has been noticed; another appears in the choir added to the Romanesque cathedral at TUAM (Galway) early in the century. There is good reason to believe that this building was begun before 1312 and was evidently part of a scheme, never completed, to rebuild the whole cathedral. Its detail is very English, flowering strangely in Connacht. This Englishness in style is, indeed, a valuable clue to the dating of the work; the Archbishop, William de Bermingham, who reigned from 1289 to 1312, was a member of a great Anglo-Norman family and a vigorous prelate. At his accession the chapter, moreover, had only one Irish member as against at least three English and two foreign (possibly Italian) canons.[4] There is other evidence still more specific. It is on record that in 1312 the dean was granted " relaxation of a hundred days of enjoined penance to those who contribute to the rebuilding of the church of Tuam begun by the late Archbishop William and continued by Dean Philip who petitions for aid to complete it."[5] The structure is a simple rectangle (71 feet by 27 feet inside) entered through a high pointed archway. To the flank and east walls are bold buttresses weathered at each stage and with foliated niches above the first weathering. These buttresses rise to a continuous corbel course, arcaded, which carried the original parapet which was, doubtless, more effectively crenellated than is the modern replacement. It is the windows, however, which deserve special notice. The east window (Pl. XXVb) is of five-light width, not a very common circumstance, even in England. (There are, however, over forty in

Exeter cathedral and it is to some of these that the Tuam example bears a close resemblance.) Each light is foliated and each side-pair has a quatrefoil centrepiece. Above the single centre-light, which is the highest, is a large circle, sex-foiled.

The whole window is deep-set in a moulded frame. Four of the six side-windows are of three lights; the others of two, and all the tracery is essentially of the same design as that in the gable but modified to suit the lesser widths.

Two other achievements of the period call for notice. Both are belfry towers and both belong to friary churches; the first—and probably the earlier—to the Dominican house at DROGHEDA, Louth, and the second to that of St. Francis in Kilkenny. With the possible exception of Buttevant (*ante* p. 110) none of the thirteenth-century friary churches had towers from the first. When these came to be built they were almost invariably inserted about midway in the length of the long and narrow edifices favoured by the mendicant orders. (This was also the case in the numerous friaries erected in the fifteenth century; most of the towers were insertions.) The method was to build two parallel walls, usually close together, across the church but not bonded into the existing side-walls. These cross-walls formed a structural barrier between choir and nave and were pierced by arched openings. The archways were usually narrow but were in some instances not greatly less in width than the church. The tower at Drogheda known as the Magdalene Tower (Pl. XXVIa) is the sole fragment remaining above ground of the church of the Dominican friary there: the thirteenth-century walls between which it was built have disappeared. The supports are relatively heavy and broad; the arches narrow but lofty and spanned by sharply-pointed arches of sandstone in several cham-fered orders. From east to west between the arches the supporting walls corbel inwards in a curve to come in line with the side-walls of the slender tower above which is but half the width of the vanished church. It is divided into two storeys externally by a weathered string-course above which the tower's width is slightly

PLATE XXIV

XXIVb.   ADARE FRIARY, " BLACK ABBEY," CHURCH

East Window of Church

XXIVa.   KILMALLOCK FRIARY CHURCH

East and South Windows of Choir

PLATE XXV

XXVb. TUAM CATHEDRAL

East Window of Choir

XXVa. THE "BLACK ABBEY" FRIARY CHURCH KILKENNY

South Window of Transept

diminished. The graceful batter of earlier and later Irish work is absent. Internally there is vaulting above the windows of the lower storey, not immediately over the main arches as became more usual. In effect the lower storey is a lantern with windows of two lights, foliated beneath a quatrefoil. The upper—the belfry—windows are

FRIARY OF ST. FRANCIS, KILKENNY: TOWER.

Restoration of parapet is conjectural.

W. ELEVATION.

SECTION E. TO W.

65

M

of the same design but are taller. Each has a transom. Documentary evidence for dating this tower is lacking but the window design is appropriate to the early fourteenth century. If this date be accepted the Magdalene Tower is the earliest stone belfry to a friary church in Ireland and, possibly, in Britain.

In the case of the second belfry tower, that at KILKENNY (65), the grounds for dating are somewhat more secure though still not definite. The friars of the Kilkenny house had extended their choir eastwards in 1321 and were, in 1347, undertaking the construction of a new " campanile." By implication there was or had been one but it may well have been of timber. In 1349 the Black Death came to the " Faire Citie " and we are left to surmise whether the tower was completed before or after the catastrophe. On stylistic evidence a mid-century date for the work is acceptable. The supporting arches are of wide span, indeed of the maximum possible width to give adequate body to the inserted piers. These are plain chamfered as are the arches above them which have a soffit rib borne by short attached colonettes rising from corbels sculptured with the figures of donors and workmen. Within is a ribbed vault of two bays, with a wall-shaft similarly supported, below the belfry floor. The tower is square in plan and narrow, very little wider than the arches which carry it. In each of its faces are two-light windows to the belfry stage. They have cusped ogee heads below a quatrefoil and are transomed. Parapets of the Irish pattern crown the walls but remain complete only at the angles.

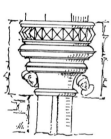

Sketch of Capital in respond to the arch of destroyed N. transept chapel.
ST. FRANCIS' FRIARY
KILKENNY
66

(The presence of a respond (66) in the outer face of the north wall at the tower shows that there was a chapel—and therefore a transept or wing—there. The capital has small monkish faces below the numerous mouldings commonly found in capitals of c. 1300.)

In earlier chapters mention has been made, more than once, of the " Irish " stepped battlements or parapets. So frequently do these crown Irish medieval buildings that the title is not undeserved but they cannot be claimed as an Irish invention; their origins must be sought further afield. Possibly, indeed probably, the introduction is datable to the fourteenth century—see the discussion of Kildare cathedral (*ante* p. 89).

Britain provides no obvious exemplars, nor does northern France; in northern Italy, it is true, stepped battlements appear occasionally, as in the massive tower near the west front of the cathedral of St. Zenone at Verona. The area in which the features are most numerous, however, is at the eastern end of the Pyrenees; the ancient French province of Roussillon (now Dept. Pyrenees-Orientales) and Catalonia immediately to the south. Rey[6] calls them *merlons-en-escalier* or *créneaux Roussillonais*. He cites the south-west Romanesque tower of Elne cathedral[7] and illustrates the defensive tower—*clocher-donjon*—of the church of Coustouges (Ariège).[8] To the south, in Catalonia, there are still more examples. The great Romanesque monastery of St. Martin-du-Canigou (*c.* 1009) has a very massive square tower north of the presbytery, doubtless an addition but of early Romanesque type. It has stepped battlements closely similar to Irish work.[9] Santa Maria de Ripoll, another Catalonian monastery church (*c.* 1090) and rather more advanced Romanesque than St. Martin, has a south-west tower with these stepped crenellations. So has a tower at Breda, also in Catalonia.[10] Ultimately, as Rey points out,[11] the source is to be found in the Irano-Syrian models of the Orient.

If the Roussillon and Catalonia be thought too remote from Ireland to affect its architectural development it should be remembered that one of the pilgrimage routes to Compostella ran across France, diagonally, from the Gironde to the south-east and thence westward, south of the Pyrenees, to the famous shrine of St. James. It is not an unreasonable surmise that Irish pilgrims may well have followed this route and have observed, on the way, these picturesque features of the hospitable monasteries so closely concentrated around the eastern limits of the mountains.

With the plague of 1349, Irish building activity seems to have ceased. It was slow to recover and very little work definitely of the second half of the century is to be found, but two examples and a possible third may be cited. The more important was the rebuilding, begun in 1372, by Archbishop Minot, of the four western bays of the north arcade of the nave of St. Patrick's cathedral in Dublin, and of the imposing tower adjoining. The four arches are higher than the originals and rise from octagonal pillars which are plain but for attached shafts to the east, west and north sides. Minot's tower, a great, square mass of grey—and in parts now black—local calp limestone, rises to a height of 147 feet (not including the granite spire of 1749) to the summit of the Irish battlements which crown the walls. In the lowest storey the walls are ten feet thick. There are four turrets, three of them of slight projection, the fourth, the staircase turret, projecting more strongly to the west. Diminishing in width at each of the weathered string-courses which divide the external height into five main storeys, this great belfry is unrivalled in dimensions by any other Irish tower (it is just 40 ft. square at the base) and combines with crude strength a grace of silhouette. The windows, whether original or of the fifteenth century, as are some of them, are small except for those of the belfry stage. These are large and have simple tracery and transoms. That on the north side is possibly the work of Archbishop Tregury (ob. 1471) and the others are restorations to the same design.

Not to scale

TOMHAGGARD. CH.

67

A minor example of the period, not certainly dated but definitely of later fourteenth-century style, is the east window of the small church at TOMHAGGARD (Wexford) (67). Its three lights have ogee heads, cusped, and switch-line tracery in which cusping produces the pointed trefoil shape as well as ordinary trefoils.

Also in Wexford is the other example of the period to be cited: the church of the Augustinian friary at CLONMINES. Of it only the choir, a short and narrow south aisle and an inserted tower remain. The nave has gone as have the mullions and tracery of the large east window. This was a very elaborate design if the sketch in Grose's *Antiquities* is to be relied on. The south windows of the choir were each of three lights as the surviving heads show. These are ogee-shaped, cusped, the central light being higher than its companions. The ogee form appears also in the ruined sedilia niches, the piscina, and in the tracery of a square-headed window on the north side now blocked by the belfry structure. Of the date of this church there can be little doubt. It is on record that Nicholas, the clerk, son of Nicholas, greatly embellished the church in 1383[12] and the design accords well with this date.

A close search through Ireland's many ivied ruins of small churches might produce some more examples of late fourteenth-century building but, on the evidence which is readily available, the three structures cited seem to complete the tale for the second half of the period. Recovery was slow but once begun it gathered strength until, in the middle of the following century, the output of new building in abbeys, friaries and churches reached a remarkably high pitch. It is to this architecture of the fifteenth century that the projected third volume of this work will be devoted.

1. Curtis: *History*, p. 96.
2. Rae: Thesis, unpublished.
3. Macalister: *J.R.S.A.I.*, 43, p. 201.
4. *Calendar of Papal Letters*, I, p. 498.
5. *ibid.*, p. 109.
6. Rey: *Les Vieilles Églises Fortifiées du Midi de la France*, Paris (1925), pp. 70-72.
7. See also Whitehill: *Spanish Romanesque Architecture*, Oxford (1941), Pl. 16.
8. Rey: *ibid.*, fig. 3.
9. Whitehill: *ibid.*, Pl. 6.
10. *ibid.*, Pl. 53.
11. Rey: *ibid.*, p. 71.
12. Hore: *History of the Town and County of Wexford*, pp. 199 ff. quoting Archdall: *Monasticon Hibernicum*, and Ware-Harris.

Chapter VIII
SOME FEATURES OF CHURCHES AND MONASTERIES

THE preceding chapters have been devoted, for the most part, to whole structures—their plans, styles and dates—and little was said about minor features of the buildings discussed. It is with such features that this chapter is concerned. Though the examples cited in it are not numerous they are, none the less, representative and are selected from a much larger number still extant.

Ambries. These small wall-cupboards are of frequent occurrence; scarcely any sanctuary but has one or more in its walls. The form is usually very simple—no more than a rectangular recess. But a few are different; at Kilfinaghta church (p. 66) there is one with a triangular head and at Drumacoo (41) are several with pointed heads. At the former church a second ambry is rectangular but both it and its companion have simple mouldings round them. Many ambries are rebated all round the margins obviously for a wooden door or shutter.

Cloister Arcades. Very few cloister ambulatory arcades of a date prior to the fifteenth century remain, even in part. So few fragments survive, indeed, that the presence of arcades in stone at many monasteries datable to the twelfth and fourteenth centuries is open to doubt. It is quite possible, however, that a timber-built, veranda-like structure may have served in many cases to give shelter to the ambulatories. On the other hand the most interesting fragment which does survive is also the earliest. It is part of an arcade at Mellifont (Pl. XXVII) reconstructed with the original stones discovered there during recent excavations. The unmoulded arches are round—Romanesque—and the work is probably coeval with the first church consecrated in 1157. The capitals and bases are blocks set across the whole width of the low base wall and are similar in design; shallowly scalloped on the lower and upper edges respectively. The effect is very continental: the simplest expression of the many more elaborate cloister arcades of Romanesque Europe. A fragment of a capital (or base) very similar to those at Mellifont has been found at another Cistercian house—Abbeyshrule, Longford.[1] The only other fragments so far found—and in this case of the thirteenth-century date—are a base and capital for twin pillars at Baltinglass abbey. Probably the arches were pointed or trefoil-pointed. Round arches can mislead the observer of Irish work. They occur, or recur at all dates. In the Jerpoint abbey arcade, for instance, they appear though it is a fifteenth-century work and therefore, beyond the scope of this volume. It is permissible to surmise, however, that in this case an earlier, round-arched arcade existed at Jerpoint and served as model for the later work. In some cases a wall, pierced by windows, takes the place of a regular arcade. This is so at Athassel priory. The windows in it are grouped in threes, have cusped-ogee heads and splay widely inwards. It is not impossible that this example belongs to the late fourteenth century.

Credences and Piscinae. These niches (see Glossary) are often combined in pairs. Where one of the pair lacks the drain which is usually found in a piscina it may be inferred that the bowl (lavabo), a movable utensil, was emptied into a drain somewhere else in the church. The simple pair at Jerpoint (Pl. XXVIIIa) has a short central pillar supporting the lintel. It has no drain but the example in the church of Fore abbey, which has two round arches, has a drain at one side. The arches, jambs and central pillar are chamfered and there are traces of simple decoration in colour on the internal plaster. The niches at Ballintober Abbey (29) closely resemble the Fore example but are much smaller and have no drain. A round-headed piscina niche at Derrynaflan calls for mention later (see p. 147).   In one of the chapels of the north transept of Kilkenny cathedral is a niche of unique form.   Its head is twice shouldered—stepped—and it is moulded at the sides and top (68).   It is a mid-thirteenth-century work.   Somewhat earlier in the century is the piscina niche in St. Mary's church at New Ross (69).   It has a moulded, trefoil-pointed arch and engaged jamb-shafts with delicate stiff-leaf capitals.   The arch form seen here is a favourite one throughout the thirteenth century and in the fifty following years; an excellently-wrought example is to be seen at St. John's priory in Kilkenny, not in the church but rebuilt as a memorial in a wall to the west of the restored building.   Another but later and much simpler niche occurs in Rathfran friary church.

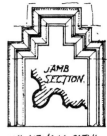

KILKENNY CATHL.
NICHE: N. TRANT. CHAP.
68

Sedilia.   These niches for clergy seats usually accompany piscinæ in the south walls of chancels.   The earliest form seems to be the single wide niche, round-headed, to accommodate a bench for the three priests.   Ballintober (29) is one example.   But the simple form never went quite out of fashion as that at late thirteenth-century Rathfran shows.   (There are also fifteenth-century examples.)   The sedilia in Corcomroe abbey church (70) though spanned by one bluntly-pointed arch enclosing similar sub-arches is not so simple as the examples so far cited.   Obviously a central pillar for the sub-arches would have made the seating of three clerics impossible; a simple corbel-capital takes the place of a pillar and leaves the seat unencumbered.

CHANCEL PISCINA
ST. MARY'S CHURCH
NEW ROSS
69

In the normal form of sedilia there are three niches.   Possibly the earliest example extant is at Jerpoint (Pl. XXVIIIa).   Each niche has a round arch with chevron decoration which continues down the jambs to the stone seat.   Many thirteenth- and fourteenth-century sediliæ have been restored but all, except the latest, are of the same form: three moulded, trefoil-pointed arches borne by jamb and intermediate, free-standing shafts of marble or fine lime-stone as in the group in St. Francis's friary church, Kilkenny (71) of *c.* 1321.   Of about the same date is the sedilia in the " Black Abbey " at Adare, and Limerick has another of 1360-1370 in the

CORCOMROE ABBEY, CLARE: SEDILIA.

70.   Corcomroe Abbey, Co. Clare: sedilia

Magdalen chapel. Its arches are trifoliated and its shafts are twisted; the capitals are of foliage and even the spandrels of the cusps are decorated. In its elaboration it contrasts with the simpler example surviving at Leighlin cathedral which is datable to

Plate XXVI

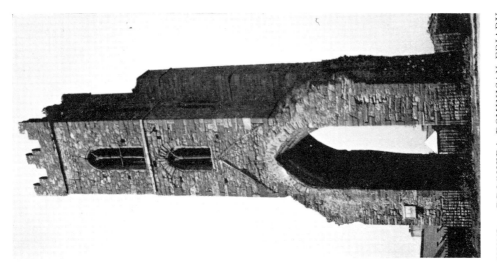

XXVIa. DROGHEDA DOMINICAN FRIARY

The Magdalene Tower

XXVIb. MELLIFONT ABBEY

Window in Chapter-house

Plate XXVII

XXVII. MELLIFONT

Original Cloister Arcade Restored

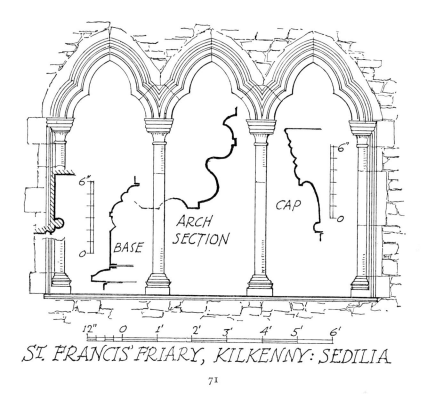

ST. FRANCIS' FRIARY, KILKENNY: SEDILIA

71

c. 1300. In general the main differences between thirteenth- and fourteenth-century sediliæ are in the details of the mouldings; the capitals in the later period show a multiplicity of small mouldings in contrast with the few and bolder members found in earlier work. Traces of an ogee-headed sedilia remain at Clonmines. Here the piscina and sedilia have been robbed of wrought stone but the form of the arches remains clear.

Tomb Niches. Many churches possess broad wall recesses for tombs. A quite usual but not invariable position for these features is in the north wall of the chancel. When near to the altar such a tomb is probably that of the noble founder or of some important benefactor. But tomb niches occur in other parts of the building; there is one such of thirteenth-century date in the north wall of the nave of Ardmore cathedral (Pl. XXVIIIb). It has a trefoiled arch, moulded, and short engaged shafts with moulded capitals. A large niche of the same period, also with a trefoiled arch but surmounted by a gable, stands in the north wall of the chancel of St. Mary's church at New Ross. Also gabled but of less certain date is the segmental-arched niche at Corcomroe. The tomb niche in the north wall of the transept of Kilkenny cathedral (Pl. XXa)—perhaps that of Bishop de Mapilton—is of mid-thirteenth-century date and is quite the finest example in Ireland. Its arch and hood-moulding, both richly moulded in contemporary style, are trefoil-pointed; well carved heads serve as stops and stiff-leaf capitals crown the marble nook-shafts. The cusps have carved bosses and the bases are of the water-holding section. While the moulded tomb slab is original, the frontal below it is of much later date. The recesses in the south aisle of Gowran church (Pl. XXVIIIc) which are of *c.* 1280, have multi-cusped arches. The workmanship, if less bold than that of the Kilkenny cathedral example, is of almost equal quality.

Rathfran friary church, not much later than that at Gowran, has several simpler niches: having merely trefoil-pointed arches with but one moulding.

In conclusion it may be said that few of the examples cited above approach the elaboration to be found in similar features of fifteenth-century churches.

1.   Information from Mr. W. P. Le Clerc.

Plate XXVIII

XXVIIIa. JERPOINT ABBEY CHURCH
Credence Seats and Piscina

b. ARDMORE
Tomb Recess Arcade

c. GOWRAN
Tomb Recess Arcade

TOMB RECESSES OF EARLY AND LATE
THIRTEENTH CENTURY

Appendix I

SHORT NOTICES OF BUILDINGS OMITTED FROM PRECEDING PAGES

There are many churches, large and small, still existing which belong to the period or contain features of it. Not all of them are as notable, however, for one reason or another as those which have appeared in the foregoing study of the subject. Some have been over-restored in modern times; others have been virtually rebuilt in the very active fifteenth century, or virtually ruined before or since that period; still others are small in size and contain but little work datable to the great period. None the less, all these structures cannot be entirely ignored here, and there follow short notices of selected examples. The arrangement is alphabetical, not stylistic, chronological, or in order of importance.

ABBEYSHRULE (Longford). In the east wall of this Cistercian abbey—colonized from Mellifont in 1150—there remain some Transitional window details and, near the centre of the church, a pulpitum structure of three compartments, vaulted. It lacks any wrought stonework.

AGHADOE (Kerry). There survive in the east gable wall of the " Cathedral " ruin two tall and narrow lights, of Transitional type, with pointed rear-arches.

ARDCATH (Meath). The nave-and-chancel church, now in ruin, is of fair size (about 110 feet in overall length) and has several single, trefoil-pointed windows of late thirteenth-century type. It had an east window of three pointed and cusped lights (fourteenth-century ?), grouped.

ARDSALLAGH (Meath) is also known as CANNISTOWN. The small nave-and-chancel church (rebuilt in the fifteenth century) retains the chancel arch of an earlier structure. The arch is semicircular, is moulded and rises from carved capitals. Both are defaced but that to the north has animals (dogs ?); the other has three demi-figures and a chalice ?[1]

BALLYBEG (Cork). The long, rectangular church of the Augustinian priory, much ruined, has a massive and late tower built within its west end partly obscuring the rear-arches of two large pointed windows. The splays of these meet in a banded

145

shaft which bears a capital of foliage with three small human faces. It resembles those to the west window of Gowran church (Pl. XXIb) but is less competently wrought. This part of the church appears to be of the late thirteenth century. On the south extensive claustral buildings, now ruined to foundation level, surround a court 90 feet square. The bases to the jambs of the chapter house doorway (three pillars in single file) remain as well as a fine shelf-like laver stone. There are numerous stone coffins in niches of the choir. A detached, round columbarium of uncertain date lies to the east-south-east.

BALLYNATRAY (Cork). The " Abbey " of Molana. Here are the ruins of a priory of Canons Regular. They consist (a) of a long, rectangular church mainly of the thirteenth century, perhaps embodying some earlier work, and (b) a cloister-court and ranges on the south. The long choir has a row of six pointed windows in the south wall and four similar lights (but further west) on the north. The chancel arch is ruined and the nave is, in part, older. In the south wall of the Frater are the remains of the reader's pulpit recess.[2]

BANNOW (Wexford). Within the area of the vanished Anglo-Norman town is the ruin of a simple nave-and-chancel church with added south and north porches. The chancel arch is round and unmoulded but the jambs below it have roll mouldings. Battlements of fourteenth-fifteenth-century date crown the side-walls. In the east wall a three-light, switch-line window (fourteenth century) takes the place of three original windows. The rear-arch is segmental-pointed and the tracery, now gone, was cusped and very similar to that of the east window at Tomhaggard church (67). There are hollow chamfers to the angles of the splays and to the rear-arch.[3] The south door is lintelled below a relieving arch.

BRIDGETOWN (Cork). The older name is Ballidroghid. Of the large priory founded in the early thirteenth century for Augustinian Canons (of the Congregation of St. Victor, as was also Newtown Trim) there are considerable remains. These comprise the church—a long rectangle—and some of the claustral ranges and courtyard. In the north wall of the choir is a range of windows of which some of the embrasures have banded shafts.

CARLINGFORD " ABBEY " (Dominican Friary). The window openings of the long, narrow friars' church (125 ft. by 22 ft. inside) are lacking in datable detail most of the cut stone having been removed. Between the short choir and longer nave there is a tower of oblong plan raised on solid side walls and carried by pointed arches of chamfered section with a rough vault between. As the access to this tower is a staircase in the south wall of the choir it would appear to be an original feature not, as is usual, a later insertion. The west wall was crenellated in the Irish fashion and has a square turret at each angle giving the structure the appearance of fortification. As it was outside the walls of the town some fortification may have been necessary. The east window was large (about fifteen feet wide) and lofty. It probably consisted of a group of lancets. Among the changes in the building is a late west door, an insertion. There are some remains of domestic buildings to the south-east. In the main the structure belongs to the fourteenth century and may date to 1305—the date of its foundation by Richard de Burgh—or soon thereafter.[4]

CARRICKFERGUS (Antrim). There remains in the large parish church of St. Nicholas, which is cruciform and originally had nave-aisles, a respond pier of the crossing. It is of Transitional (c. 1185) plan: a pointed member flanked by bold rolls. This is paralleled in Byland and Roche Abbeys, Yorkshire. In the nave-walls are traces of arcades with round arches borne by cylindrical columns crowned by multi-scalloped capitals of everted section.

CLOMANTAGH (Kilkenny). A parish church, in ruins, of rectangular plan. It has two lancets in the east wall and other pointed lights in the side-walls.[5]

DERRYNAFLAN or LURGOE (Tipperary). The remains of the church of this small monastery, situated on a bog island central in the county, consist of the east, north and south walls of the chancel. A short but wider nave is represented only by foundations. Five windows, two in the east wall and three (two paired) in the south wall, are the features of interest. Each is a small, single light, trefoil-pointed, chamfered and rebated externally and splaying widely inwards. The rear-arches are segmental, very slightly pointed. A round-headed piscina niche with very shallow mouldings, including beadings, around it, perhaps comes from an earlier church.

DOWNPATRICK (Down). The cathedral church of Down, dedicated to the Holy Trinity, is the choir of the Benedictine house founded by John de Courcy in 1183, after he had expelled the Canons Regular installed there by St. Malachy. The building is not of the twelfth century but an addition to a church probably of that period. No vestige of that church remains, however; its form and dimensions are unknown but there is no reason to believe that it was cruciform or very large. The size of the choir and the fact that it has coextensive aisles suggest that it was part of an ambitious scheme (as that later one at Tuam, p. 131) to rebuild the whole edifice on a large scale. Aisled choirs are of unusual occurrence in Ireland—the two Dublin cathedrals are the only other examples—and it may well be that the relative grandeur of the Down structure is due as much to the large ideas of the Benedictines as to Anglo-Norman pride and liberality.

The history of the cathedral is unfortunate. So early as c. 1220 the structure was in a bad way; in 1245 is it said to have been damaged by an earthquake and in 1538 it was again destroyed. This destruction was obviously partial since the carcase was still standing, roofless, when restoration was begun about 1790. This considerable undertaking was completed about 1826 by the erection of a tower at the west end and connected to it by a short vestibule. The restoration was drastic and included much refacing of walls and re-tooling of wrought stonework. It was in the " revival " style then prevailing which was based upon superficial knowledge of medieval architecture. As a consequence analysis and definitive dating of the original work is very difficult. Indeed, it still remains to be done.

DUBLIN. St. Audoen's Church. The only medieval church still standing in the city. Of the original building, altered and enlarged into a double-aisled church in later centuries, only the nave belongs to the period. It is roofed and in use. A round-headed doorway of *c.* 1190 in the west wall remains from the first church but the built-up arcade of four bays in the south wall has pointed arches, rather ineffectually moulded, and shafts of eight half-column plan. A date late in the thirteenth century may be assigned to this arcade. The fifth bay, to the east, which has square piers, is of later date. All the nave-windows on the north side are timber-framed and of the nineteenth century. The switch-line east window is a modern restoration.

DUNGIVEN (Derry). The choir of the Augustinian priory church is mainly of the twelfth century and the nave apparently about two centuries later in date. A wide round-topped arch, moulded, separates the two. In the east wall are two narrow, round-headed lights. Moulded wall-ribs in the chancel, carried by corbel capitals in the four corners, suggest that it was vaulted or that vaulting was intended. In the chancel, on the south side, is the elaborate canopied tomb of the O Cahan (Cooey nGall) who died in 1385 " at the pinnacle of prosperity and renown."[6] Its arch and hood-mould (the latter with a row of beading, like small nail-heads) enclose a tympanum of curvilinear tracery. This is carried by a semi-circular arch member in the same plane, multi-cusped. The effigy slab is moulded and has a row of beads. It surmounts an altar-form base with an arcade frontal of six trefoil-headed niches, strongly moulded. In each niche is a figure of a gallow-glass warrior in strong relief. It is possible that this rich work belongs, as is generally believed, to the late fourteenth century. If this be so it is the first of a fine series of canopied niches with Flamboyant tracery in other parts of Ireland which were made in the following century. The whirling, cusped, " comma " shapes within circles of the Dungiven example remind one of the inserted east window at Jerpoint Abbey (61) but the work more probably belongs to the fifteenth century and is, therefore, outside the chronological scope of this volume.

FENAGH: E. WINDOW

72. Fenagh Abbey Church: east window

FENAGH (Leitrim). The " abbey " church here is mainly remarkable for a Geometrical Decorated east window (72) of four pointed, cusped lights below a circular centre-piece of six pointed trefoils around a central eye and flanked by similar trefoils. All the cusps are of the soffit type and the eye truncates one foil in each aperture. The window is probably of the fourteenth century but conceivably may be later.

FURNESS (Kildare). This very simple nave-and-chancel church (about 55 feet long inside) is remarkable in that all the dressings are of a local calcareous tufa. The chancel arch is semicircular, unmoulded, with heavy, chamfered imposts to the square jambs. The widely splayed embrasures of the single side-windows of the chancel and nave (one to north and south in each) are round-topped and in the east wall there is a pair of small, round-headed lights with a central mullion. The three west windows are almost destroyed and the north and south doors of the nave have lost most of their dressed stonework. In the south wall of the chancel near the dividing wall there is a " low side-window " (erroneously a leper's squint), the only Irish example of this feature observed. The church was evidently built to serve an Anglo-Norman estate and was granted by Richard de Lesse, the owner, to the Abbey of St. Thomas, Dublin, in 1210. It is probably datable to about that time.[7]

GALWAY, St. Nicholas. In this, the largest medieval parish church in Ireland and mainly of late date, there are two-light windows south of the chancel and a three-light, switch-line window in the north transept. All the lights have pointed arch-bars at the springing and all these windows appear to be fourteenth-century, forerunners of types which were to become common later. The nave arcades also appear to belong to the 1300's and with one exception, the pillars, arches and responds resemble those to the north aisle of Claregalway friary church. In the south wall of the south transept, which was extended in the sixteenth century, is a fine, three-light window, obviously re-erected, with curvilinear tracery of fourteenth-century design.[8]

INISFALLEN (Kerry). In the east gable of the chancel added to the largest church of the group (Vol. I, p. 68), which has some claustral buildings attached on its north side, there are two simple, very narrow lancets. The south light has been restored.

KILKENNY. St. Mary's Church. This large cruciform church, originally aisled, is an erection of the thirteenth century. It has been greatly modernized.

KINSALE (Cork). The church of St. Multose is one of the few medieval parish churches in Ireland still in use. Though much altered and restored in parts it is very much, in extent and plan, as when first built in the early thirteenth century. It is a rectangular building, originally divided by a cross-wall into nave and chancel, with north and south aisles and a small north transept arm. The north aisle extends eastwards to nearly the end of the chancel from a massive, low tower at the north-west angle. All but one of the plain, very heavy, square piers and pointed arches of the seven-bayed arcade on this side were removed in 1835.

The exception is the west arch which supports the tower. It shows the original form. The south aisle is to the nave only. It has four pointed arches springing from piers less massive than were those of its vanished counterpart.

Two arches to the chancel-aisle on the north are modern. Also relatively modern (early nineteenth-century) is the low pitched roof spanning both nave and aisles in place of the original three roofs of steeper pitch. There is reason to believe, on the evidence of one Transitional, pointed window-head now built into the north face of the tower, that the earliest work may be of the early thirteenth century. It is not impossible that this fragment is from one of the original east windows. The group of three lancets in the west wall, however, is apparently of mid-century date (the east window is a modern copy of it); the groups of three or five lights in other parts of the church are less certainly datable.[9]

KILFINAGHTA (Clare). The church is an early building (possible of c. 1080) but has two windows of Transitional—and western—type framed all round with triple rolls (cf. Banagher, p. 65). An ambry framed in a roll moulding is triangular-headed and has another below it square-headed and moulded there and at the sides only.[10]

LOUGHREA (Galway). Simple lancet windows still prevail in Irish work so late as c. 1300 which is the approximate date of the foundation of this Carmelite friary. The ruined church has been renovated and contains windows of fifteenth-century style in addition to the lancets.

LOUTH " ABBEY " (Dominican Friary). All the claustral buildings, which lay to the north of the church, have gone but its end-walls, south side-wall and a short piece of the north wall remain to nearly full height. It is long and narrow (154 ft. by 26 ft. 4 ins. inside) typically a friars' church. A cross wall divided a long choir from a shorter nave. The only datable features are the remains of the much damaged windows. The east window, apparently of four lights set in a deep casement, had complex tracery of switch-line pattern with foiled apertures (cf. south window of " Black " abbey, Kilkenny, Pl. XXVa and Fig. 59). It is built within the built-up aperture of a much larger window—original or intended—perhaps of seven grouped lancets (cf. St. Francis' Friary, Kilkenny, Fig. 56). Three of the six south windows had three lights and plain, switch-line tracery. The west window was similar. There are moulded quoins to the east wall. Since all the mullions and bars are rebated as well as chamfered and the arch stones and jambs moulded, a fourteenth-century date for the work is probable.[11]

MARLFIELD (Tipperary). A fine round-headed doorway of Transitional detail from the long-demolished Cistercian abbey of Inislounaght (" de Surio ") close by is preserved in the west wall of the modern parish church. Other details of later date are to be seen, re-used, in the windows of the same church.

MONAINCHA (Tipperary). This twelfth-century church (Vol. I, pp. 129-36) was altered in the middle of the following hundred years by the insertion, in the south wall of the nave, of two windows in the new fashion. The external trimming has gone but segmental-pointed rear-arches remain. The jambs have delicate angle-shafts with carved capitals in which small heads appear. The east window, of which less remains, was also widened in the same period and style. (See *J.R.S.A.I.*, Vol. 50, Fig. 4.)

MOVILLA (Down). On the site of the eighth-century monastery there is a long rectangular church, much ruined, of thirteenth-fifteenth-century dates. Near the east end of its north wall are two lancets set close together, widely splayed inwards and united by an external hood-moulding. The most notable feature is the built-up east window of *c.* 1300. It is of three lights with uncusped switch-line tracery. The mullions, tracery bars and jambs are hollow-chamfered and have external rebates. Set low in the centre-light is a small round-headed window from a much earlier building.

NEWTOWNARDS (Down). The surviving arcade of the nave of the ruinous church of the Dominican friary, a mid-thirteenth-century foundation, is very similar in detail to that at Claregalway and, like it, appears to be a fourteenth-century work.

NEWTOWN TRIM (Meath). The priory was founded in 1206 by Simon de Rochfort, Bishop of Meath, for Canons of the Augustinian Order following the Rule of the Congregation of St. Victor of Paris. It was to serve as a cathedral for the diocese. Of the church only the choir-walls and those of parts of the nave remain. The nave was reduced in length in the later Middle Ages when, apparently, the transept and nave-aisles were removed. The choir windows were tall lancets, having banded shafts within, and set between broad pilaster-form buttresses. This part of the structure either had, or was intended to have, vaulting. Later thirteenth-century capitals and shafts remain in the south wall of the nave near its west end. Of the claustral buildings which were situated to the south-west on lower ground sloping to the bank of the river Boyne, little more than the south and west walls of the frater remain. This apartment was raised on an undercroft. It has windows of mid-thirteenth-century style.

OLD ABBEY (Limerick). The ruin of a long rectangular church dating to the earlier thirteenth century remains. It belonged to a convent for Augustinian nuns. There is a good pointed west door with moulded and pillared jambs, moulded arch and a hood-moulding. Also surviving is the walled cloister court curiously situated west of the church and axial with that structure. There are the ruins of the late thirteenth-century refectory and later kitchen on the south and of under-vaults of the domestic buildings on the west of the court.[12]

QUIN (Clare). Parish church of St. Finghin. This plain, aisleless building with no marked internal division is datable to the earlier part of the thirteenth century. In the perfect east gable are three lancets, the highest in the centre, chamfered and rebated externally and widely splayed inwards. Most of the north wall is gone; the south-west turret and the eastern buttresses are additions.[13]

RATHKEALE (Limerick). The Augustinian priory church at Rathkeale is a long rectangle, of the type usually favoured by the friars. It had a west tower and the nave had a short north aisle. There are five lancets, four close-set, in the south wall of the choir, and a door and an archway, further west, led to the demolished cloister. There were originally three lancets in the east gable where there is now a four-light switch-line window of the fifteenth century.[14]

ROSCONNELL (Kilkenny). A much-altered church, rebuilt in part in the seventeenth century and probably altered in earlier times, which has a small and attractive late thirteenth-century east window. This is of three trefoil-pointed lights (73) graduated in height and width.

½ OUTSIDE　　½ INSIDE
ROSCONNELL CH. E. WINDOWS

73

SHANAGOLDEN (Limerick). The nave-and-chancel church of the thirteenth century has a Transitional (*c.* 1200) east window. On each side of the nave are arcades of four bays with unmoulded piers and pointed arches. They are closed externally by later walls; apparently the aisles intended were not built or, if built, have been demolished.[15]

TOMFINLOUGH (Clare). This early church, partly rebuilt *c.* 1300, has a two-light south window with moulded jambs and rear-arch. There are capitals of low relief foliage carving of the Transitional, western type. The heads of the lights are pointed and there was a moulded central shaft.[16]

TRINITY ISLAND, Loch Cé (Roscommon). The overgrown remains of the Premonstratensian priory founded before 1250 call for closer and more critical examination than they have yet received. The simple church has very narrow lancet windows, perhaps never glazed.[17]

TRIM (Meath). Little more than the belfry of the great Augustinian priory church of St. Mary survives. Even the belfry has lost most of its western half and south face, but the rest stands to its full height of 125 feet; a noble remnant and a landmark locally known as the Yellow Steeple. It is square in plan and sited on the north side of the demolished church. There are angle turrets, also square (cf. Minot's Tower, St. Patrick's Cathedral, Dublin, also of the fourteenth century) diminishing in width at the weathered string-courses which mark each of the four external stages. The walls, however, are not battered but rise vertically. Internally there were seven storeys of which the lowest has a barrel-vault. The surviving window in the belfry stage is of two lights with a transom and simple curvilinear, uncusped tracery.

TRISTERNAGH (Westmeath). Of the very important Augustinian priory, founded *c.* 1200, only two bays of the west end of the church remain embedded in domestic work of post-Dissolution date. Two octagonal pillars carrying scotia-moulded capitals and chamfered arch rings indicate a fourteenth-century date for this part of the church.

YOUGHAL (Cork). St. Mary's church. This, the second largest parish church of medieval times still standing and in use in Ireland, is mainly of mid-thirteenth-century date. The long chancel, however, belongs to the fifteenth century and replaces a probably shorter original chancel. There is much restoration, particularly about the windows, but no essential change of the original character. The plan is cruciform, with aisles to the nave and a short west aisle to the north transept. In the arcades the piers are square and the pointed arches unmoulded. On the north side there are five bays plus a wider arch to the transept and in the south arcade there are six equal bays. There was a rood-loft approached by a stairs, still existing, in a broad pier south of the chancel archway but the corresponding pier of similar dimensions on the north has gone. The chancel arch is in two orders. Its piers have bold angle-shafts, attached, bordered by deep hollows flanked by rolls. Most notable features of the church are the triple and paired pointed lights of the transept windows. (Incidentally, it is interesting that these windows are repeated in the later chancel varying only in the carved detail which is obviously of fifteenth-century style and date.) In the west gable is a tall triplet, original, and below it a doorway in two orders with jambs similar in section to the first order of the chancel but on a smaller scale and with small, unattached shafts. A massive, fortress-like tower stands detached on the north in the re-entrant of the nave and transept.

1. Crawford: *J.R.S.A.I.*, Vol. 51 (1921), pp. 125-32.

2. Power: *J.R.S.A.I.*, Vol. 62 (1932), pp. 142-52.

3. Hore: *History Town and County of Wexford*, Vol. IV, pp. 444-57. Also Du Noyer *Proc. R.I.A.*, VIII, p. 64, and *R.I.A. Drawings*, III, 61-2.

4. Davies: *County Louth Archæological Journal*, X (1941-42), pp. 103-6 and Pl. I.

5. Carrigan: *History Diocese of Ossory*, Vol. II, pp. 366-9.

6. Ann. Four Masters and Loch Cé.

7. Synott: *Jour. Kildare Arch. Soc.*, Vol. III (1902), pp. 457 ff.

8. Leask: *Jour. Gal. Arch. and Hist. Soc.*, Vol. III (1936), pp. 1-23.

9. Darling: *The Church of St. Multose.* Pamphlet.

10. Westropp: *Proc. R.I.A.*, 3rd Ser., Vol. VI, No. 1, p. 151, Pl. XI, 5 and 9.

11. Davies: *County Louth Archæological Journal*, X (1941), pp. 8-10, and *J.R.S.A.I.*, XXVIII, pp. 314-16.

12. Westropp: *Proc. R.I.A.*, Vol. XXV, Sec. C, No. 8, p. 395, Pls. XI and XV.

13. O Brien: *Arch. and Topographical Record* (1905), Vol. I, Pt. 2.

14. Westropp: *ibid.*, p. 391.

15. Westropp: *ibid.*, p. 396, Pl. XVIII.

16. Westropp: *Proc. R.I.A.*, Vol. VI, No. 1, p. 149, Pl. XII.

17. Rae: Thesis, unpublished.

GLOSSARY

Abacus (Pl. Abaci).   The horizontal member above the capital of a pillar or column.

Ambry or Aumbry.   A cupboard in the thickness of a wall generally near to an altar.

Ambulatory.   A walk or passage, such as a cloister walk or an aisle passing behind the high altar at the east end of a chancel or choir.

Apse.   A half-circular or polygonal termination of a church or of a chapel therein.

Arcade.   A series of arches on pillars or columns.

Arch.   See the different forms in Fig. 74.

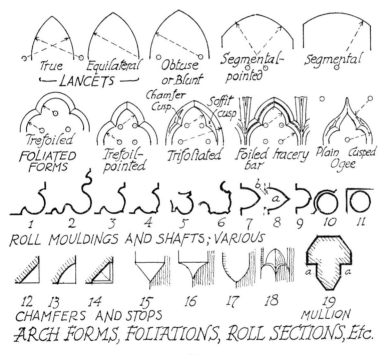

74

Arris.   A sharp angle or edge, usually square or so slightly rounded as not to merit the name of moulding.

Ashlar.   Squared, finely finished masonry.

155

Back- or Rear-arch.   An arch spanning the inner embrasure of a window or door opening. Sometimes called scoinsion or sconcheon (among several alternative spellings) arch. (This peculiar term applies more strictly to the side surface of an embrasure.) See also Drop-arch.

Ball-flower.   A decorative motive—a globular flower of three petals enclosing a small ball or bead—much used in English architecture of the first quarter of the fourteenth century (64).

Batter.   Inward sloping of the face of a wall or quoin.

Bead.   A narrow **Bead.**   A narrow, rounded moulding.

Bowtell.   A roll moulding. Fig. 74, 2 to 6.

Casement.   A recess in a wall surface round about a window opening.

Chamfer.   A splayed or bevelled surface made by cutting off a square edge. Fig. 74, 12 to 14 for forms.

Chancel.   The eastern arm of a church. So called because it was originally cut off from the nave by screens, **cancelli.**

Chapter House or Room.   The apartment in monasteries set apart for the daily meetings of the brethren at which a chapter (**capitulum**) of the Rule of the Order was read. In later buildings the meeting place of the chapter: the governing body of a cathedral church.

Choir.   In a church the space set apart for the monks, canons or friars or, separately, for the lay brethren. The monks' choir usually extended westwards into the nave and terminated, eastwards, at the eastern arch of the crossing. East of this were the presbytery and the sanctuary, q.v. See also Fig. 4: plans of Cistercian churches.

Clearstorey or Clerestory.   Part of a building with windows above the roof of a lower, adjoining part, e.g., in a church, the nave windows above the aisle roofs. Pl. XIa and Figs. 8, 20, 43.

Colonette.   A narrow pillar or vertical pillar-like moulding.

Corbel.   A stone projecting to support something over it. Often in the form of a capital. Figs. 25, 26, 44.

Corbel shaft.   A combination of a corbel-capital with a short, engaged wall-shaft. Figs. 16, 30.

Credence.   A table or shelf for the elements and utensils of the Mass, the lavabo bowl, etc. Survives in Ireland as a piscina-like niche or niches. Pl. XXVIIIa, Figs. 29, 68.

Crocket.   A spur- or hook-shaped foliage ornament at intervals along the coping of a gable or the like.

Crossing.   In cruciform plans the space coincident with the transept. It is sometimes covered by a tower.

Cusp.   One of the inward-projecting points forming the foils (q.v.) in medieval window-heads, arches, panels, etc. The two main forms are the chamfer and soffit cusp. Fig. 74.

Dog-tooth.   An ornamental motive typical of thirteenth-century work. It is made up of pyramidal flowers of four petals. The nail-head motive (q.v.) is similar, smaller and usually uncarved. Fig. 75.

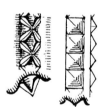

"DOG-TOOTH" AND "NAIL-HEAD" ORNMTS.

75

Dressings or Trim.   The wrought, finely finished stonework about an angle, quoin, window or doorway, etc.

Drop-arch.   Back arch of which the apex is below that of the external window.

Engaged Shaft.   A shaft, usually of about three-quarter-round section, attached to and part of a pillar or wall-face.

Fillet.   A narrow nib or projection wrought on a roll or other moulding or shaft. Fig. 74, 4, 5, 6.

Foils and Foliation. Foil. A leaf (Lat. pl. folia); a leaf-shaped lobe, round or pointed. Foliation: the practice of foiling arches or other openings (as in tracery). A foiled arch or opening is one made up of several foils; a trefoiled arch enclosed in a pointed arch is said to be trifoliated. Foliation is usually produced by cusping, however. Fig. 74 shows selected examples.

Groin. In vaulting the line of intersection of two vault surfaces—soffits—at an angle to one another.

Groin-rib. A stone arch rib on the line of or supporting a groin. It is therefore a diagonal rib in any bay of vaulting. The other vault ribs are the transverse- or cross-ribs and the wall-ribs, both of the same shape and span as the vault. The wall-ribs are where the vault abuts upon the wall.

Hood-moulding, label, or dripstone. A projecting member, usually moulded, over an arch or lintel.

Impost. The plane in which an arch rests upon a pillar or pier.

Impost moulding. A horizontal member marking an impost.

Jamb. The side of an archway, doorway, window or other opening.

Label. See Hood-moulding.

Lancet. A long narrow window with a pointed head. The term is specifically applied to the form most sharply pointed but often also to windows with an equilateral arch. Fig. 74.

Low-side-window. A small window close to the floor-level in a chancel wall near its western end. Popularly but erroneously a "leper's squint" but more probably used for the ringing of the Sanctus bell.

Merlon. The solid part of an embattled parapet between the notches or crenellations.

Mullion. A vertical dividing bar in a window, usually chamfered, sometimes also rebated and in some cases with an engaged, narrow roll or shaft at the nib or point. Fig. 74 (19).

Nib. The narrow point of a mullion.

Nook-shaft. A detached shaft set in a nook or recess. Fig. 74 (10, 11).

Offset. A setting back of the face of a wall.

Ogee. A compound—reversed—curve partly convex, partly concave. Fig. 74 of ogee-headed window.

Order. One of the series of the jambs and concentric arches of an opening, adjacent to and stepping back from one another.

Presbytery. The eastern part of a monastic church, east of the monks' choir and extending to the sanctuary. Fig. 4.

Piscina. A basin for washing the sacred vessels. It is provided with a drain and is usually set in a small niche in the wall of the sanctuary or chapel near to and south of the altar. Fig. 69.

Quoin. The external angle of a building or part thereof, such as a buttress.

Rear-arch. See Back-arch.

Rebate. A continuous rectangular recess cut in the edge of a solid. Fig. 74 19, " a."

Respond. A half column, pier or pilaster which projects to carry an arch, expecially at the end of an arcade. Figs. 22, 36, 51.

Sedilia (Sing. Sedile). Seats, usually three together, in the south wall of a chancel or sanctuary for the use of the priests during the Mass. Pl. XXVIIIa, Figs. 29, 70 and 71.

Skewback. A stone with a sloped upper surface forming a base for an arch. More loosely, the lowest voussoir of an arch.

Soffit. The under-surface of an arch, lintel or projection.

Soffit-rib. An arch-rib beneath a soffit. Fig. 44.

Spandrel. A triangular compartment or space.

Springing. The starting point of the curve of an arch.

Spur Ornament. Carved leaf or other form at the base of a round pillar on a square plinth or base-block. Figs. 10, 11.

Still-leaf foliage. This type of foliage sculpture is characteristic of thirteenth-century capitals, etc. In essential it consists of stylized trefoil leaves usually simple and stiff in early examples, curling boldly outwards and sideways in those of later date. (In the nave of Christ Church Cathedral, Dublin, however, this stage was reached early in the century.) Figs. 42, 49, 52, 54 and 76.

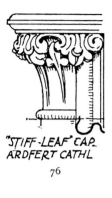

"STIFF-LEAF" CAP.
ARDFERT CATHL
76

Stop. (a) The shaped termination of a chamfer; (b) projecting stone at the termination of a hood-mould carved as a knot of ornament or a human head. A mask-stop roughly resembles a human face. Pl. XXa.

Torus. A moulding of bold, round section in or at the base of a pillar. Fig. 11.

Tracery. See Pls. XXIIIb, XXIVb, XXVa and b, Figs. 58 to 62, 67, and 72.

Transept. The cross-arm of a church; strictly, in the singular, the whole arm but often applied to each part separately, i.e., " North Transept," " South Transept." Loosely any wing projecting laterally from a church fabric.

Transom. A horizontal bar in a window. Fig. 65.

Triforium. The usually arcaded blind-storey coincident with the aisle roof, above the nave arcade and below the clearstorey. Pls. XI, XII. Fig. 43.

Tympanum. The stonework enclosed within an arch over a door or window. Pl. XIX.

Voussoir. One of the wedge-shaped stones composing an arch.

Wallplate. A piece of timber lying on a wall-top to receive the feet of rafters.

BALLYBEG ABB.
W. WINDOW.
ARDFERT CATHL.
WATER-HOLDING
BASES.
77

Water-holding base. A base with a bold outward and upward-facing hollow between the small upper and lower larger rolls. Typical of the thirteenth century, especially of the first half. Fig. 77.

Weathering. Sloping of the upper surface of a coping, sill, string- or base-course, or offset of a buttress, etc.

INDEX

Numerals in heavy type indicate the pages in which will be found the more important and detailed information about individual buildings, etc., more general and cross references are in ordinary type. Italic numerals refer to the drawings in the text and Roman type to the Plates.

Abbreviations : Pry., Priory ; Fry., Friary ; Abb., Abbey ; fdr., founder ; Bp., bishop ; Archbp., archbishop ; Knts., knights ; poss., possible ; Cathl., cathedral ; Ch., church.

A—BUILDINGS AND PLACES

Abbeyshrule, Longford, **145**.
Adare Fry. Ch., " Black Abbey," Limerick,
            126. 141 ; XXIVb.
do. Trinitarian Ch., do., 23.
Aghadoe " Cathl.", Kerry, **145**.
Annaghdown, Gal., 26.
Ardcath Ch., Meath, **145**.
Ardfert Cathl., Kerry, **111-13** ; *55 ;* XXb.
do. Fry., do., **113-14** ; XXIa.
Ardmore Cathl., Wat., **39-40**; XXVIIIb.
Ardsallagh Ch., Meath, **145**.
Athassel Pry., Tipp., 20, 21, 81, 101, **94-99** ;
            48, 49.
Athenry Fry. Ch., Gal., **93-94**, **126-28** ; *57, 58.*

Ballintober Abb. Ch., Mayo, 63; 67; *29, 30.*
Ballybeg Pry., Cork, **145-6**.
Ballynatray Pry., Cork, **146**.
Baltinglass Abb., Wick., 8, 12, 17, **26-8**, 29,
            30; *4, 5.*
Banagher Ch., Derry, **65-6** ; *32.*
Bannow Ch., Wex., **146**.
Bective Abb., Meath, 17.
Boyle Abb., Roscommon, 8, 10, 13, 15, 26.
    32-5, **61-3**, 75, 92; *4, 9, 10, 11, 12, 13* ; I, II.
Breda (Catalonia), 135.
Bridgetown Pry., Cork, **146**.
Buildwas Abb., Salop, 28, 43, 47.
Buttevant Fry., Cork, **110-11**, 132.
Byland Abb., Yorks., 49.

Cannistown Ch. (see Ardsallagh).
Carlingford Fry., Louth, **146-7**.
Carrickfergus Ch., Antrim, **147**.
Cashel Cathl., Tipp., **89-93**, 96, 103; *47 ;*
            XIIIb, XVI, XVII.
do. Domn. Fry. Ch., do., **93**, 96, 101, 110.
do. Hore Abb. (see Hore).
do. Teampull Chormaic, 3, 89.
Castledermot Fry. Ch., Kild., 94, **125-6** ;
            XXIIIb.
Cistercian church plan, 6 ff., 13; *4.*

Claregalway Fry., Gal., **94**, **130** ; *63.*
Clomantagh Ch., Kilk., **147**.
Clonfert Cathl., Gal., **71-2** ; *38,* frontispiece.
Clonmacnoise, Temple Ri, Off., 59.
Clonmines Fry. Ch., Wex., 22, **136-7**, 143.
Cloyne Cathl., Cork, 118 ; XXII.
Cong Pry., Gal., **59-61**, 63, 75; *28 ;* VIIb, VIII.
Corcomroe Abb., Clare, 10, 13, **58-9** ; *23 ;*
            VI, VIIa.
Coustouges (Dept. Ariège, France), 135.

Derrynaflan, Tipp., **147**.
Devenish Pry., Ferm., 67.
Dore, Hereford, 43.
Downpatrick Cathl., Down, **147-8**.
Drogheda, Magdalene Tr., Louth, **132-3** ;
            XXVIa.
do. Ch. of St. Peter (destroyed), 117.
Drumacoo Ch., Gal., **73-6**, *40, 41 ;* IX, X.
Dublin, Abbey of St. Mary, 47, 83.
do. Ch. of St. Audoen, 117, **148**.
do. Cathl. of " Christ Church," 20, 34,
    39, **43-5**, 55, **77-81**, 82, 85, 87, 88,
    92, 105, 116; *20, 42, 43 ;* IV, XIa.
do. Cathl. of St. Patrick, 49, 83, **81-2**,
          105, 125, **136** ; *43 ;* XII.
Dunbrody, Abb., Wex., 6, 15-16, 32, 49, **83-4**,
          85, 88; *44;* XIb.
Dundalk, Ch., of St. Nicholas, Louth, 117.
Dungiven Pry. Ch., Derry, **148**.

Elne Cathl. (Dept. Pyr. Or. France), 135.
Ennis Fry., Clare, **118-20** ; *56.*
Erinagh Abb., Down, 19, 48.
Exeter Cathl., Devon, 132.

Fenagh, Leitrim, **148-9** ; *72.*
Ferns, Cathl. of St. Aidan, Wex., **99-101**.
do. Augustinian monastery, 26.
Fethard " Abbey," Tipp., **129** ; *60.*

Fore Abb., Westmeath, 20, **47.**
Furness Ch., Kildare, **149.**

Galway, Ch. of St. Nicholas, **149.**
Glendalough, Wicklow, 20, 64.
Gowran Ch., Kilk., **116-17** ; XXIb, XXIIIa, XXVIIIc.
Gracedieu Nunnery, Dublin, 23.
Graignamanagh Abb., Kilk., 6, 8, 15, 16, 32, 34, 35, 83, 85, **86-9,** 105; *4, 46;* XIV.
Grey Abbey, Down, 8, **49-51,** *23 ;* V.

Holy Cross Abb., Tipp., 6, 10, 15, 17.
Holm Cultram Abb., Cumbd., 49.
Hore Abb., Cashel, Tipp., 13-15, 91, **115-16; *4.***

Inch Abb., Down, 6, 15, **47-9 ; *4,* 22.**
Inchcleraun, Longford, 72; *39.*
Innisfallen Abb. Ch., Kerry, 149.
Inishmaine Abb. Ch., Mayo, 63, **66-8,** 71; *33, 34, 35.*

Jerpoint Abb., Kilk., 5, 7, 9, 10, 12, 14-16, 20, 26, 28, **29-32,** 87, 129; *6a and c, 7, 8, 61 ;* XXVIIIa.
Kells Pry., Kilk., 21, **99.**
Kilcooly Abb., Tipp., 6.
Kildare, Cathl. of St. Brigid, **89,** 135; XVa.
Kilfenora, Cathl. of St. Fachnan, **54.**
Kilfinaghta Ch., Clare, **66,** 149.
Kilkenny Domn. Fry. Ch., **128-9 ;** *59 ;* XXVa.
  do.   Cathl. of St. Canice, 87, **103-8 ;** *50, 51 ;* XVIII, XIX, XXa.
  do.   Fry. of St. Francis, **93-4,** 124-5, 132, **133-4,** 141; *65, 66.*
  do.   Pry. Ch. of St. John, 106, **109-10,** 124-5; *53, 54 ;* XVb.
  do.   Ch. of St. Mary, 117, **149.**

Killaloe, Cathl. of St. Flannan, **54-59 ;** *24, 25, 26, 27.*
Killone Nunnery Ch., Clare, 23, **63-4 ;** *31.*
Kilmacduagh, Gal., 20.
  do.   O Heyne's Ch., **68-71 ;** *36, 37.*
Kilmallock Fry., Limerick, 119, **120-1, 130 ;** *64 ;* XXIVa.
Kinsale, Ch. of St. Multose, Cork, **149-50.**
Kirkstall Abb., Yorks., 43.
Knockmoy Abb., Gal., 15, 32, **37-9,** 61, 63; *16, 17, 18.*

Leighlin (see Old Leighlin).
Limerick, Cathl. of St. Mary, **45-7,** 141; *21.*
Llandaff Cathl., Glam., 34, 61.
Loch Cé (see Trinity Isd.).
Lorrha Fry., Tipp., **115.**
Loughrea Carm. Fry., **150.**
Louth Fry., **150.**
Lurgoe (see Derrynaflan).

Marlfield Ch., Tipp., **150.**
Mellifont Abb., Louth, 1, 3-4, 6, 8, 11, 15-17, 32, 35, **41-3,** 61, 67, 83, 129; *3, 62 ;* III, XXVII.
  do.   Lavabo, 40, 41; *19 ;* XXVIb.
Molana " Abbey " (see Ballynatray).
Monaincha Ch., Tipp., **151.**
Monasternenagh or Manister Abb., Lim., 8, 10, 15, 16, **35-38,** 59, 70; *4, 6b* and *c, 14, 15.*
Movilla Ch., Down, **151.**

Nenagh Fry., Tipp., **114.**
New Ross, Ch. of St. Mary, Wex., 34, **85-6,** 88, 90, 101; *45 ;* XIIIa.
Newtownards Fry., Down, **151.**
Newtown Trim Fry., Meath, 22.
Newtown Trim Pry. (Cathl.), Meath, **151.**

Old Abbey, Lim., **151.**
Old Leighlin Cathl., Carlow, **126,** 142.
" Ossory, Convent of," 29.

Pershore Abb. Ch., Worcs., 79.
Pipewell Abb., Northants., 43.

Quin Ch., Clare, **152.**

Rathfran Fry., Mayo, **117-18.**
Rathkeale Pry., Lim., **152.**
Ripoll, Santa Maria de, Abb. (Catalonia), 135.
Roche Abb., Yorks., 49.
Roscommon Fry., **114-15.**
Rosconnell Ch., Kilk., **152 ;** *73.*

St. Martin-du-Canigou (Catalonia), 135.
Salisbury Cathl., Wilts., 81.
Shanagolden Ch., Lim., **153.**
Sligo Fry., **115.**
Stanley Abb., Wilts., 43, 86.
Strata Florida Abb., Card., 86.

Thomastown Ch., Kilk., **117.**
Tintern Abb., Mon., 121.
Tintern Minor Abb., Wex., **121.**
Tomfinlough Ch., Clare, **153.**
Tomhaggard Ch., Wex., **136,** 146; *67.*
Trim, Pry. of St. Mary, Meath, **153.**
Trinity Island Abb., Loch Cé, Rosc., **23.**
Tristernagh Pry., Westmeath, **153.**
Tuam Cathl. choir, Gal., **131-2 ;** XXVb.
  do.   Abb., Ch., Gal., **72-3,** 75.

Verona (St. Zenone Cathl. Tower), 135.

Waterford Fran. Fry., **94.**
Wells Cathl., Somerset, 34.

Youghal, Ch. of St. Mary, Cork, 117, **153-4.**

INDEX 161

B—SUBJECTS AND PERSONS

For authors and sources cited or quoted—in addition to those referred to in
" Acknowledgments "—see notes at the end of each chapter

Affreca, wife of de Courcy, 49.
Aidan or Maidoc, St., Bp. of Ferns, 101.
Alexander IV, Pope, 22.
Altar, nave, 12.
Ambries, 66, 75, 139, 155; *41.*
Ambulatory, 12, 14, 16-17.
Anglo-Norman foundations, number of, 4.
  do.   extent of dominion, 77.
Apsidal plan, 8.
Arcades of cloisters, 17, 31, 139; XXVII.
Archdall, Mervyn, 20, 39.
Arch forms, etc., 155; *74.*
Arrouaise, Congr. of, 43.
Athenry, battle of, 1316, 123.
Augustinian Canonesses, 23.
Augustine, St., Canons Regular of, 20, 21, 79, 80.
  do.   Hermits of (Austin Friars), 22.

Ball-flower ornament, 129-30, 156; *64.*
Barry, de, fdr. Buttevant Fry., 110.
Base, Water-holding, 158; *77.*
Basil, St., 2.
Belfry towers, absence or presence of, 8.
  do.   inserted, 132-3.
Benedictine Order in Ireland, 1, 20, 147.
  do.   Rule, 2, 19.
  do.   poss. first church at Jerpoint, 20, 28.
Bermingham, de, lords, 123.
Bermingham, Wm. de, Archbp. of Tuam, 131.
Bernard, St., of Clairvaux, 2, 3, 8.
" Black Death," plague, 123-4, 134.
Bristol Channel, 76.
  do. stone from, 85.
Bruce, Edward, 81, 123.
Burgh, de, fdr. of Rathfran, 117.
  do.   lords, 123.
  do.   Walter, 96.
  do.   William, 97.
Butler, lords, 123.

Calefactory or Warming House, 15.
Carmelite Order, 22.
Carnsore Point, 76.
Chapter House, 14-5.
Chevron ornament, 39, 41, 45; 64, 75-6; *20, 31.*
  do. late survival of, 53, 75-6.
Christian, Bp. of Ardfert, 111.
Cistercian Nuns, 23.
  do. Order, system, etc., model plan, 4, 5, 6, 8 ff.
Citeaux, 2.

Clairvaux, 2-3.
Clare, Richard de, " Strongbow," 43.
Clearstorey, 156.
  do. windows, incidence of, 10.
Cloister arcades, 14.
  do. court or garth, 14.
  do. open passage west of, 17, 43.
Comyn, John, Archbp., 81, 103.
Credence niches, 140, 156; *29, 68 ;* XXVIIIa.
Courcy, John de, 20, 47, 51.
Crenellations, stepped, 89, 92, 113, 117.
  do. origins, *créneaux Roussillonais,* 134-5.
Crutched Friars, 22.
Curia (outer court), 6.

Day stairs, 15.
Dervorgilla, 3.
Dog-tooth ornament, 156; *75.*
Dominican Order, 21.
Dorter (dormitory), 15.

East (dorter) range, 14-5.
Eva, dau. of MacMurrough, 84-5.
Evreux, Abb. of St. Taurin, 47.

fitzGerald, lords, 123.
  do. Maurice, Justiciar, 115.
fitzStephen, Robert, 43.
Franciscan Order, 21.
Franciscans, Third Order of, 22.
Frater (refectory), 15-16.
  do. Lay, 16.

Gate-houses, 6.
le Gros, Raymond, 43.
Guinness, Sir Benj. Lee, 82.

Hackett, Bp. of Ossory, 108.
Harding, Abbot Stephen, 2.
Henry of London, Archbp. of Dublin, 81, 103.
Hospitallers, Order, 23.

Ileyan, Maurice, Bp. of Kilmacduagh, 68.
Infirmary, 6, 43.
Innocent II, Pope, 3.
  do. IV, Pope, 22.
Isabel, Marshall, ctss. of Leinster, 84.

John, prince, later king, 55.

Kitchens, 15.
Knox, Bp. of Killaloe, 58.

Lacy, Hugh and Walter de, 47.
Lancets, persistence of, 124, 157; *74.*
Laura, earliest monastic form, 1-2.
Lavabo or Laver, 16, 40-41, 146.
Lay-brethren (*conversi*), 5, 6.
    do.   Choir of, 10, 12; *2, 4.*
Lecterns, 10, 14.

MacCarwill, David, Archbp. of Cashel, 89-90, 115.
MacJordan, fdr. Rathfran, 117.
MacKelly, David, Archbp. of Cashel, 81, 91, 93.
MacLochlain, Murteach, High King, 4.
MacGillapatrick, King, 29.
MacMurrough, Dermott, King, 26, 84, 101.
Malachy, St., Bp., 2, 3.
Mapilton, Hugh de, Bp. of Ossory, 103, 105, 107.
Marshall, Wm. the Earl, 84, 86, 89, 121.
Mendicant Orders, 21.
Merlons-en-escalier (see Crenellations).
Minot, Archbp. of Dublin, 81, 136.
Monks (*monachi*), 5.
    do.   choir of, 10.
Monte Cassino, 2.
Montemarisco, Geoffrey de, 99.
Montmorency, Hervey de, 83.

Nicholas fitzNicholas, 137.
Necessaria (latrines), 16, 99.
Night stairs, 10.
Novice House, 15.

O Brien, Donal Mór, King, 46, 53-5, 64, 89.
    do.   Donat, 53.
O Brien's victory (1318), 123.
O Brien, Marianus, Archbp. of Cashel, 89.
    do.   Turloch, king, 119.
O Cahan (Cooey nGall), 148.
O Carroll, Donogh, prince, 3, 4.
O Conor, Cathal Crovderg, king, 53, 63.
    do.   Felim, lord of Roscommon, 114.
    do.   Roderick, son of Cathal, 53.
    do.   Maelisa, prior, 67.
O Duibhe-rathra, Moel-ettrim, Bp., 39.
O Hedian, Archbp. of Cashel, 90-91.
O Heyne, Owen, 71.
O Kennedys, fdrs. of Nenagh, 114.
O Maicen, Maelbrighe, Abbot, 63.
O Ruairc of Brefini, 4.
O Toole, Lawrence, Archbp. of Dublin, 43.

Perpyn walls, 11-2, 29; *8.*
Philip, dean of Tuam, 131.
Piscinae, 118, 140-1, 143, 157; *68, 69.*
Pointed arch, first appearance of, 25.
Premonstratensian Order, 23.
Presbyteries, 10; *2, 4.*
Processional doorways, 14, 28, 35, 49, 85; *46;* XIV.
Pulpit of Reader, 15, 50, 89.
Pulpitum, 12.

Retro-choir, 10.
Robert, French monk-architect, 8.
Rood, The, 12, 97.
    do.   Loft, 10.
Roscrea, See of, 54.
Roussillon, anc. province, 135.

Sacristy, 14. See plans, *2, 4, 29, 37, 48.*
St. John, John de, Bp. of Ferns, 83, 87, 10.0.
St. Leger, Geffrey, Bp. of Ossory, 103, 105
Santiago de Compostella, 135.
Scattery (Iniscathy), See of, 54.
Screens, wooden, 12.
Sedilia, 118, 141-3; *29, 70, 71;* XXVIIIa.
Sitric " Silkbeard," King of Dublin, 43.
Stalls, wooden, 11, 12.
" Stiff-leaf " foliage, 158; *76.*
Stone, import of, 77, 85.
    do.   limestone, use of, 90, 105.
Sunday procession, 12, 43.
Switch-line tracery, 110, 125-28; *58a, 59, 60;* XXIIIb.

Syrian origins, supposed, 66.

Templars, Order of Knts., 23.
Tomb niches, 143-4, 148; XXa, XXVIIIb & c.
Tracery, definition and types of, 124-5; *59, 65, 72.*
Trefoil (pointed), 127, 136; *60, 67, 72.*
Tregury, Archbp. of Dublin, 136.
Trinitarian Order, 23.
" Turn " or Latch, 16.

Viking Terror, 1, 19.
Ware, Sir James, 20, 54.
West range, uses, 16.
Windows framed in mouldings, 38, 56, 63-66. 71; *16, 27, 30, 32, 38,*